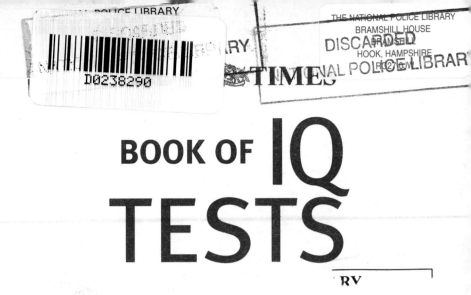

BOOK OF IQ TESTS

RV

THE TIMES

BOOK OF IQ TESTS

top uk mensa puzzle editors

ken russell and philip carter

book 2

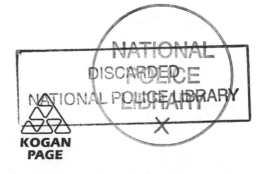

**KOGAN
PAGE**

First published in 2002

Kogan Page Limited
120 Pentonville Road
London N1 9JN
UK

Kogan Page US
22 Broad Street
Milford CT 06460
USA

The views expressed in this book are those of the authors, and are not necessarily the same as those of Times Newspapers Ltd.

British Library Cataloguing in Publication Data

A CIP record for this book is available from the British Library.

ISBN 0 7494 3733 2

Typeset by Saxon Graphics Ltd, Derby
Printed and bound in Great Britain by Clays Ltd, St Ives plc

Contents

Introduction

Intelligence quotient (IQ) is an age-related measure of intelligence and is defined as 100 times the mental age. The word 'quotient' means the result of dividing one quantity by another, and intelligence can be defined as *mental ability* or *quickness of mind*.

An intelligence test (IQ test) is, by definition, any test that purports to measure intelligence. Generally such tests consist of a graded series of tasks, each of which has been standardized using a large, representative population of individuals. This procedure establishes the average IQ as 100.

It is generally believed that a person's IQ rating is hereditary and that the rate of development of a person's mental age remains constant until about the age of 13 years, after which it slows up. Beyond the age of 18 little or no improvement is found.

Tests that measure the IQs of children are standardized and an average score is recorded for each age group. Thus a child of 10 years of age who scores the results expected of a child of 12 would have an IQ of 120, calculated as follows:

(mental age/chronological age) $\times$ 100 = (12/10) $\times$ 100 = 120

However, because little or no improvement in IQ rating is found in adults, they have to be judged on an IQ test whose average score is 100 and their results graded above and below this norm according to known scores.

During the past 25–30 years IQ testing has been brought into widespread use by employers because of their need to ensure that they place the right people in the right job from the outset. One of the main reasons for this in today's world of tight purse strings, cost cutting and low budgets is the high cost of errors in employing the wrong person for a job, including the cost of readvertising and interviewing new applicants and of reinvestment in training.

As IQ is hereditary, it is not possible to increase your IQ. It is, nevertheless, possible to improve your performance on IQ tests by practising the many different types of question and by learning to recognize the recurring themes. The questions in this book are typical of the type and style of question that you are likely to encounter in actual tests and are designed to provide valuable practice for anyone who may have to take this type of test in the future. It is our belief that by practising different types of IQ tests, and by attuning your mind to the different types of questions you may encounter, it is possible to improve by a few vital percentage points. It is these few percentage points that may prove crucial in increasing your job prospects and may mean the difference between success or failure when attending one of the many job interviews that include an IQ test.

The tests that follow have been newly compiled for this book and are not, therefore, standardized, so an actual IQ assessment cannot be given. However, there is a guide to assessing your performance at the end of every test, and there is also a cumulative guide for your overall performance on all 10 tests.

A time limit of *90 minutes* is allowed for each test. The correct answers are given at the end of every test and you should award yourself one point for each correct answer. Calculators may be used to assist in solving numerical questions if preferred. Use the following table to assess your performance:

One test

Score	Rating
36–40	Exceptional
31–35	Excellent
25–30	Very good
19–24	Good
14–18	Average

Ten tests

Score	Rating
351–400	Exceptional
301–350	Excellent
241–300	Very good
181–240	Good
140–180	Average

It should be pointed out that intelligence tests only measure one's ability to reason. They do not measure the other qualities that are required for success, such as character, personality, talent, persistence and application.

A person with a high IQ has a better chance of success in life than a person with a low IQ, but only if that person applies himself or herself to the tasks ahead diligently and with enthusiasm. Someone with a relatively low IQ but with a high sense of achievement and great persistence can fare better in life than someone with a high IQ.

Cynics will say that the only thing having a high IQ proves is that the individual has scored well on an intelligence test. An IQ test, however, remains the only known and tried method of measuring intelligence. Some technical weaknesses do exist. Nevertheless it must be stressed how commonplace IQ tests have become, and that proficiency at IQ tests can improve one's employment prospects and give a good start to one's chosen career.

Test One: Questions

1.

To which hexagon below can a dot be added so that both dots then meet the same conditions as in the hexagon above?

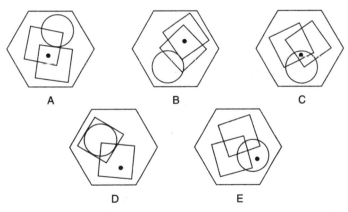

A   B   C

D   E

2. 473982 is to 1419
and
329684 is to 1418
therefore
751694 is to ?

3. Which word in brackets is closest in meaning to the word in capitals?

   ESPOUSAL
   (reverence, adoption, outbreak, opinion, invitation)

4. Solve the anagram in brackets to complete the quotation:

   Writing about music is like dancing about
   (ERECT HAIRCUT).

5. 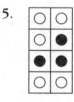 is to: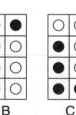

   as: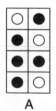

   is to:

   A   B   C   D   E

6. What is the meaning of sedition?

    a. responsive to stimuli
    b. inducing calmness
    c. relating to drinks
    d. rebellious speech or action
    e. deposit of rock fragments

7. Which number is the odd one out?

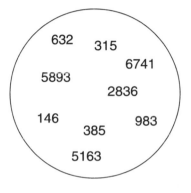

8. Start at one of the corner letters and spiral clockwise round the perimeter and finish at the centre letter to spell out a nine-letter word. You must provide the missing letters.

*	A	R
M	L	*
I	*	I

9.

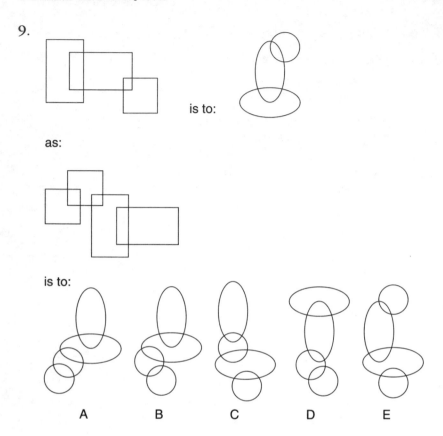

is to:

as:

is to:

| A | B | C | D | E |

10. Which is the odd one out?

bow, portal, rose, bay, lancet

11. 975, 319, 753, ?

What continues the above sequence?

12.

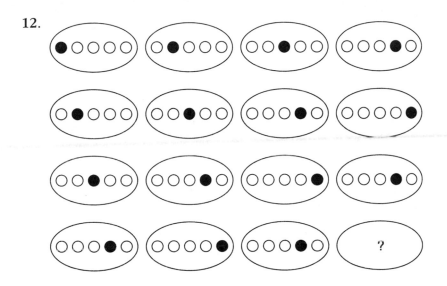

Which ellipse should replace the question mark?

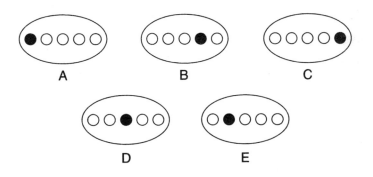

13. What phrase is indicated below?

*ND *ARCE*

14.

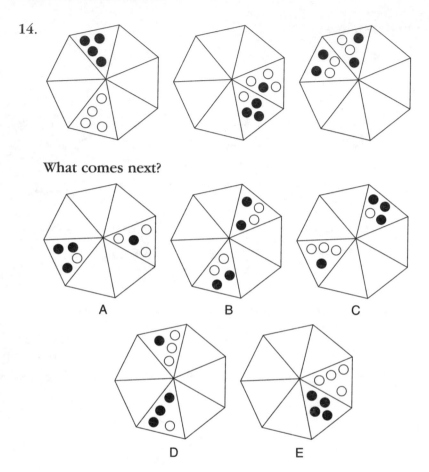

What comes next?

15. FIFTEEN DREAMS is an anagram of which two words that are opposite in meaning?

16. A sculptor starts carving a block of marble weighing 140kg. After one week he has chipped away one-tenth of the marble. After the second week he has chipped away a further two-thirds and in the final week he has chipped away 20 per cent of what he has left, by which time his work is finished. What is the weight of the final statue?

17. WITHERS is to NECK as HOCK is to:

    tail, ankle, mane, leg, hoof

18. Which is the odd one out?

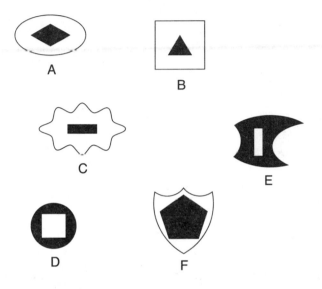

19. What number should replace the question mark?

3	8	4	9
2	4	3	6
6	7	8	2
4	2	1	?

20. Use each letter of the newspaper headline below once each only to spell out the names of three animals.

    GREAT ROTTING HEAP

21. Make a six-letter word out of these four letters.

    E R N U

22. Find a one-word anagram for

    TRIBAL ACE

23. Place two three-letter bits together to make a six-letter word that is a BIRD.

    FAL LET COM CUC COR KOA NET AIG DOR CIG

24. Which is the odd one out?

    a. ESCUDO
    b. HELLER
    c. TESTER
    d. BUSKIN

25. Find a nine-letter word by moving from letter to letter in any direction. Each letter must only be used once.

A	N	I	D
K	B	R	U
O	C	L	D
Z	M	T	E

Clue: OK to drink.

26. The combined age of Archibald and Bertie is 19. The combined age of Archibald and Charlie is 37. The combined age of Bertie and Charlie is 52. How old is:

    Archibald?
    Bertie?
    Charlie?

27. Find the trite saying by Robert Benchley.

GET	MARTINI	WET	OF
AND	THESE	DRY	A
OUT	INTO	LET'S	CLOTHES

28. Find the word, clockwise or anti clockwise.

    Clue: a motoring term.

29. Which pentagon should replace the ?

A, B, C or D?

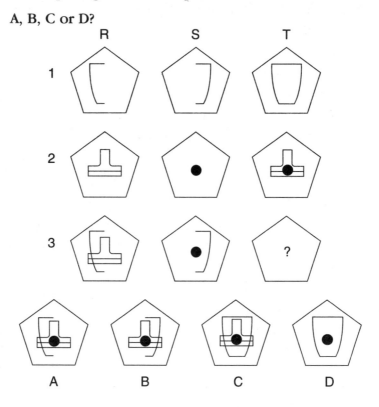

30.

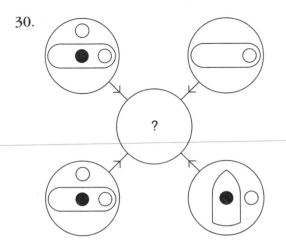

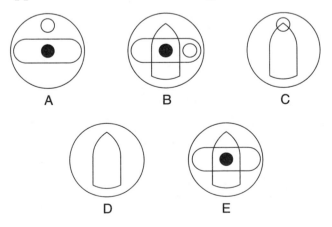

Each line and symbol that appears in the four outer circles, above, is transferred to the centre circle according to these rules. If a line or symbol occurs in the outer circles:

- once: it is transferred;
- twice: it is possibly transferred;
- three times: it is transferred;
- four times: it is not transferred.

Which of the circles A, B, C, D or E shown below should appear at the centre of the diagram above?

15

31. Change MILK to WINE, one letter at a time, in four steps.

    MILK

    ——

    ——

    ——

    WINE

32. What is a synonym for pique?

    turpitude, curtail, irritate, petulant, disfigure, disrupt

33. Find the word.

    – – FTW – – – –

34. Which two words are antonyms?

    nefarious, languid, lambent, satire,
    attenuated, copious, unchaste, decent

35. Find this trite saying.

36. Fill in the blanks to find two words that are antonyms, clockwise or anti-clockwise.

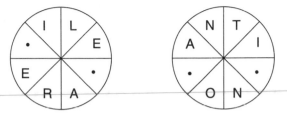

37. At the dog show the dogs' numbers were:

    corgi – 11
    alsatian – 20
    terrier – 16
    wolfhound?

    What was wolfhound's number?

38. How many different arrangements can you make of all the seven letters in the word COMBINE?

39. Trace the letters across the chords and around the circumference to find two words.

Clue: grave shapes (8–8)

40.

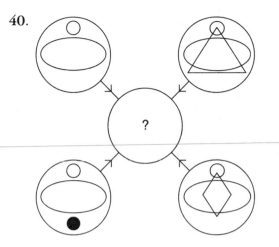

Each line and symbol that appears in the four outer circles, above, is transferred to the centre circle according to these rules. If a line or symbol occurs in the outer circles:

- once: it is transferred;
- twice: it is possibly transferred;
- three times: it is transferred;
- four times: it is not transferred.

Which of the circles A, B, C, D or E shown below should appear at the centre of the diagram above?

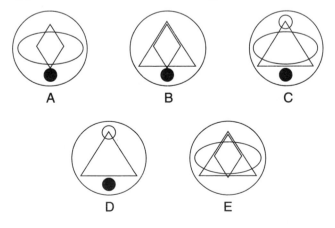

Test One: Answers

1. C; so that one dot is in both squares and the other dot is in both squares and the circle.

2. 1319 (7 + 5 + 1 = 13, 6 + 9 + 4 = 19)

3. adoption

4. architecture

5. D; the top four dots swap places diagonally as do the bottom four dots.

6. d. rebellious speech or action

7. 983; the remaining numbers are in pairs where they are reversed and the largest digit discarded – ie 5893/385, 6741/146, 2836/632, 5163/315.

8. impartial

9. B; the whole figure rotates 90 degrees anti-clockwise, rectangles change to ellipses and squares to circles.

10. portal – it is a type of door; the rest are windows.

11. 197; the numbers 97531 are being repeated in the same order.

12. D; looking across and down the black dot is moving one place from left to right, then back again when it reaches the end, at each stage.

13. part and parcel

14. A; at each stage the black dots are moving three places clockwise and one dot changes from black to white at each stage. The white dots are moving two places anti-clockwise at each stage and one dot changes from white to black at each stage.

15. same, different

16. 33.6 kg

17. ankle

18. B; it is a straight-sided figure inside a straight-sided figure. The rest are all straight-sided figures inside curved-sided figures.

19. 6; $3 \times 8 = 24$, $6 \times 7 = 42$, $4 \times 9 = 36$, therefore $8 \times 2 = 16$

20. panther, tiger, goat

21. runner

22. calibrate

23. aiglet

24. d. Buskin (a boot). Remainder are units of currency.

25. drinkable

26. Archibald 2, Bertie 17, Charlie 35

27. Let's get out of these wet clothes and into a dry Martini.

28. camshaft

29. C

30. E

31. MILK, MILE, MINE, TINE, WINE.

32. irritate

33. LUFTWAFFE

34. nefarious, decent

35. What the world needs is more geniuses with humility, there are so few of us left.

36. literate, ignorant

37. 18; consonant = 1, vowel = 4.

38. 7, or $7 \times 6 \times 5 \times 4 \times 3 \times 2 \times 1 = 5040$.

39. Egyptian pyramids

40. B

Test Two: Questions

1. Which is the odd one out?

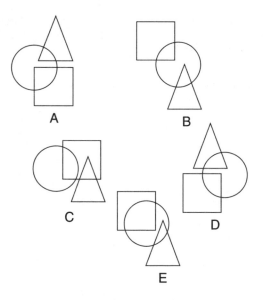

2. What number should replace the question mark?

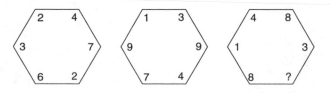

3. Which word in brackets is closest in meaning to the word in capitals?

    PORTENTOUS
    (domineering, angry, miserable, menacing, pretentious)

4. Falcon, lapwing, ostrich, cuckoo.

    Which bird below is required to complete the group of birds above?

    osprey, buzzard, vulture, kestrel, eagle

5. Which is the odd one out?

    whim, caprice, vagary, quirk, foible

6. How many lines appear below?

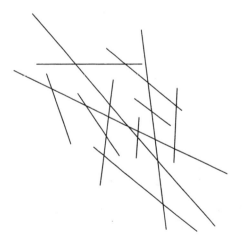

7. What number is missing?

   38 (1924) 96

   64 (3217) 68

   48 (?) 56

8. Change just one letter in each word to find a familiar phrase.

   LAID ON COD

9. Which is the odd one out?

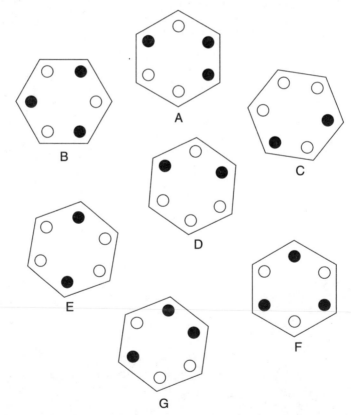

10.

A	F	E	X	T	R	A
R	A	K	I	A	M	R
E	L	I	F	T	E	B
D	T	L	O	S	E	I
N	E	D	E	A	D	T
I	R	N	E	I	E	E
K	T	A	L	L	R	R

Find two words that are antonyms. The words may appear horizontally, vertically or diagonally, but always in a straight line.

11. Which is the odd onc out?

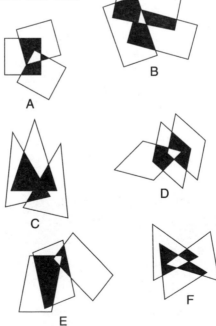

27

12. Sally had a third again as many as David, who had a third as many again as Francis. Altogether they had 111. How many did each have?

13. DAY THEATRE is an anagram of which common phrase (2,3,5)? (Clue: on your marks.)

14. BONA FIDE is to genuine as DE FACTO is to:

    assumed, together, actual, assumed, reason

15.

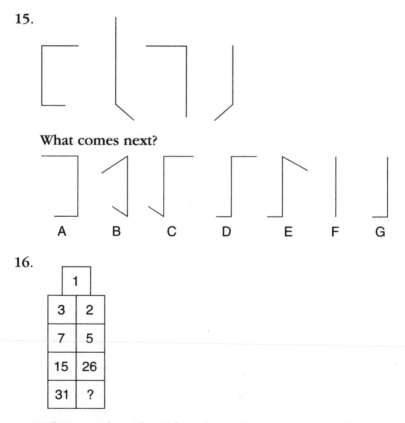

What comes next?

| A | B | C | D | E | F | G |

16.

1	
3	2
7	5
15	26
31	?

What number should replace the question mark?

17. The following clue leads to which pair of rhyming words?

    Examine place of worship.

18. Only one group of five letters below can be arranged to form a five-letter English word. Find the word.

    TACPU

    LEABO

    TCINA

    LIUDT

    CRIKD

19.

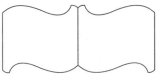

is to:

as:

is to:

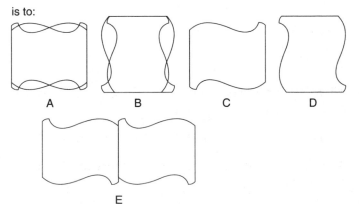

A   B   C   D

E

20. How many minutes is it before 12 noon if 12 minutes ago it was three times as many minutes past 9 am?

21. What do these words have in common?

    chubby

    boiled

    produce

    scared

    recognize

22. What is a synonym for PLATITUDE?

    humiliate, mollify, flexible, blithe, churlish, banality, character, fusty

23. Find the word.

    – – C K S T R – – –

24. What is the name given to a group of POCHARD?

    a. bunch

    b. business

    c. covert

    d. flock

25. All the vowels have been omitted from this trite saying. See if you can replace them.

    LLTHN GSBNG QLFTP RSNSS MRSPT HNTHN PRSN

26. Find five dogs, in any direction, but only in straight lines.

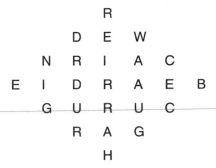

```
            R
        D   E   W
    N   R   I   A   C
E   I   D   R   A   E   B
    G   U   R   U   C
        R   A   G
            H
```

27. The combined age of Alice and Barbara is 132. The combined age of Barbara and Catherine is 152. The combined age of Alice and Catherine is 142. How old is:

    Alice?

    Barbara?

    Catherine?

28. Arrange these 12 items into three sets of three: animals, birds, insects

    DUNNOCK

    COLIBRI

    KATYDID

    APHIDES

    JUMBUCK

    BUNTING

    BULCHIN

    HEXAPOD

    MACAQUE

29. Find the highest scoring Scrabble word out of these tiles.

30. Which hexagon should replace the ?

A, B, C or D?

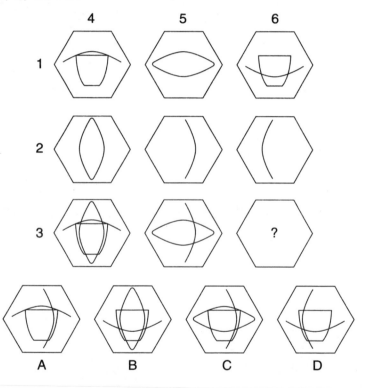

31. Simplify and find value for x.

$7 + 26 \times 29 + 8 \div 2 = x$

32. Which is the odd one out?

    a. BARBET

    b. ARNICA

    c. COLEUS

    d. IBERIS

33. Place two four-letter bits together to equal a RIVER

    OURI BLUE NALE CHIN NHAH

    COLO RADI DWAN SAVA MISS

34. Which two words are antonyms?

    relinquish, excuse, claim, scorched, spasm, indulgence, analogy, lineage

35. How many revolutions must the largest cog make in order to bring the cogs back to their original positions?

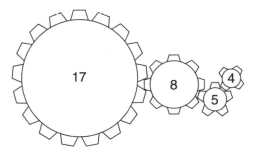

36. Fill in the blanks to find two words which are antonyms, clockwise or anti-clockwise.

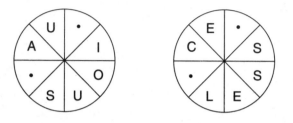

37. What is the name given to a group of swine?

    a. gang

    b. earth

    c. doylt

    d. dray

    e. hunt

38. Find a one-word anagram for

    IS A CHARM

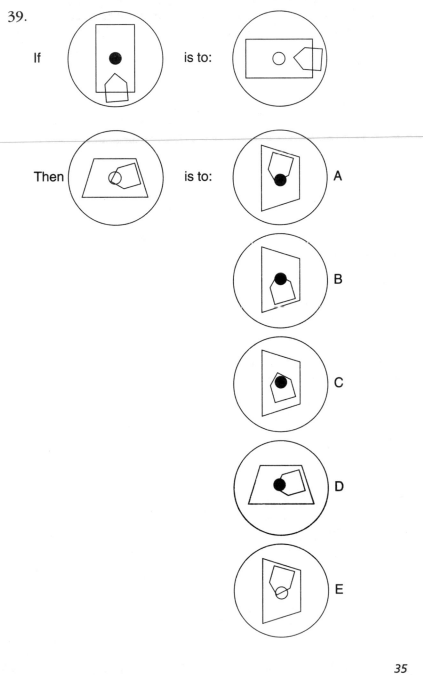

39.

If   is to:

Then   is to:

A

B

C

D

E

40. Trace the chords across the circle and around the circumference to find a word.

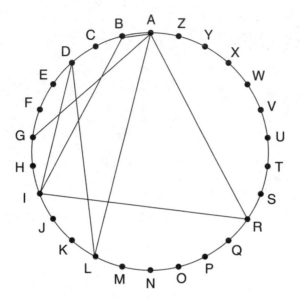

Clue: this soldier takes the biscuit! (9)

Test Two: Answers

1. C; in all the others the triangle and circle overlap, as do the circle and square.

2. 6; $418 \times 2 = 836$, as $197 \times 2 = 394$ and $236 \times 2 = 472$

3. menacing

4. Kestrel; take the first letter of each to spell FLOCK, which is the name for a group of birds.

5. quirk; quirk is an action or mannerism, the rest are odd or fanciful notions.

6. 12

7. 2414; $48/2 = 24$, $56/4 = 14$

8. Land of Nod.

9. E; A is the same as G, B is the same as F and C is the same as D.

10. resent, like

11. C; in all the others only the portions common to two figures are shaded. In C the central portion common to all three figures is also shaded.

12. Francis 27, David 36 and Sally 48

13. At the ready.

14. actual.

15. D; the top portions moves 90 degrees anti-clockwise at each stage and the bottom portion moves 45 degrees clockwise at each stage.

16. 677; down the first column, starting at 1 the sequence is double plus 1 (ie, $1+1+1=3$, $3+3+1=7$, $7+7+1=15$, $15+15+1=31$) down the second column starting at 1 the sequence is number squared plus 1 (ie, $1\times1+1=2$, $2\times2+1=5$, $5\times5+1=26$, $26\times26+1=677$).

17. search church.

18. TCINA = antic

19. C; the right figure folds on top of the left figure.

20. 42 minutes

21. They all carry a motoring term: HUB, OIL, ROD, CAR, COG.

22. banality

23. JACKSTRAWS

24. a. bunch

25. All things being equal, a fat person uses more soap than a thin person.

26. HARRIER – BEARDIE – CAIRN – RUG – CUR

27. Alice 61, Barbara 71, Catherine 81.

28. Animals: jumbuck, macaque, bulchin

    Birds: bunting, colibri, dunnock

    Insects: katydid, hexapod, aphides

29. shyly (14)

30. D; 1 is added to 2 to make 3; 4 is added to 5 to make 6; but like symbols disappear.

31. $7 + (26 \times 29) + (8 \div 2) = x$

    $7 + (+ 754) + (4) = 765$

32. a. barbet (dog). The remainder are flowers.

33. **Missouri**

34. **relinquish, claim**

35. 40

36. cautious, reckless

37. c. doylt

38. charisma

39. A

40. Garibaldi

Test Three: Questions

1.

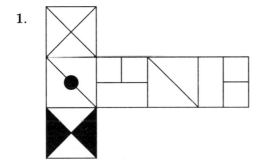

When the above is folded to form a cube, which is the only one of the following that can be produced?

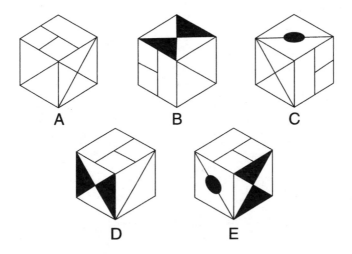

2. Find two words that are synonyms. One word reads either clockwise or anti-clockwise round the outer circle and the other reads in the opposite direction in the inner circle. You must provide the missing letters.

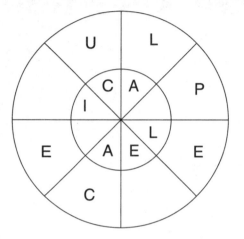

3. On the last day of his vacation a backpacker walks 40 miles, which raises his daily mileage on his backpacking vacation from 32 miles to 33 miles. How far would he have needed to walk on the final day to bring his average daily mileage up to 35 miles?

4. What is the meaning of rialto?
    a. theatre
    b. market place
    c. place for recreation
    d. bridge
    e. arena

5. Which is the odd one out?
    waltz, hornpipe, foxtrot, polka, quickstep

6.

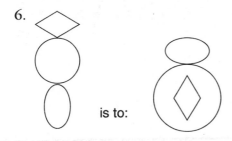

is to:

as:

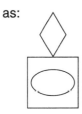

is to:

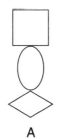   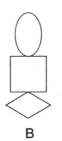   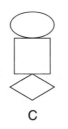      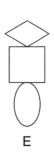

| A | B | C | D | E |

7. What number should replace the question mark?

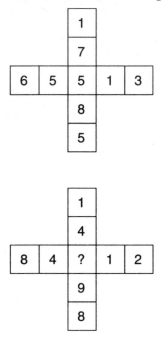

8. Add one letter, not necessarily the same letter, to each word at the front end or middle, to find two words that are similar in meaning.

    past sick

9. Billy is to goat as Jack is to:

    kangaroo, deer, donkey, ferret, polecat.

10.

What comes next in the above sequence?

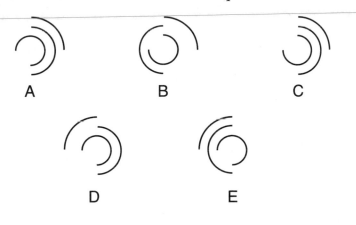

A   B   C

D   E

11. Which two numbers, one in the top circle and one in the bottom circle, are the odd ones out?

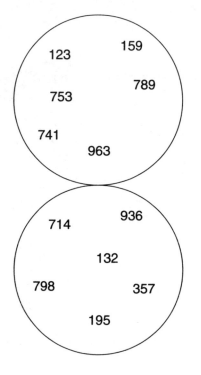

12.

Which pentagon below is most like the pentagon above?

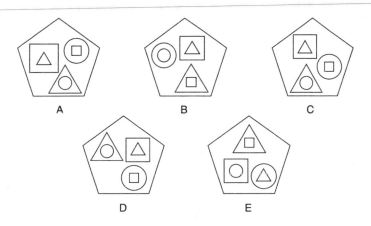

13. Which of the following is not an anagram of a type of dance?

VOTE TAG

TONGA

AVENGE

ROB LEO

TIN EMU

14.

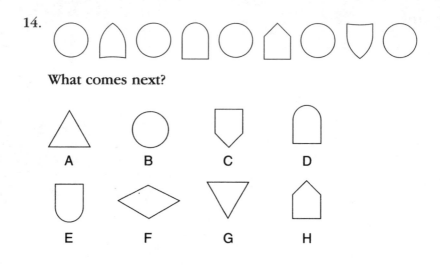

What comes next?

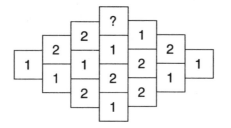

15. What number should replace the question mark?

		?		
	2	1	1	
2	1		2	
1	1	2		1
	2	2	1	
	2	2		
		1		

16. A familiar phrase has been split up and jumbled into three letter groups. Find the saying.

For example: FIND THE QUOTE could be jumbled up into DTH OTE FIN EQU

DBU EYE LED BRI DAN TAI SHY GHT

17. CAR CALLOUT is an anagram of which 10-letter word?

18.

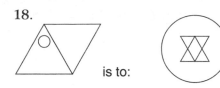 is to: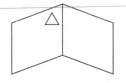

as:

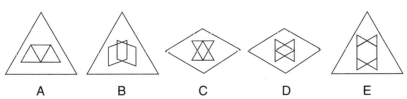

is to:

A	B	C	D	E

19. What number should replace the question mark?

4328

8567

3124

54?9

20. Insert two letters into each bracket so that they finish the words on the left and start the words on the right. The letters inserted should spell out a six-letter word when read downward in pairs.

HO (* *) ST

SH (* *) EN

MU (* *) SS

21. Place two three-letter bits together to equal a colour.

    SIE CHE OON PUR IGA

    IND NNE PLI RRI MAR

22. What is the fear of fog?

    a. homichlophobia

    b. acrophobia

    c. nosophobia

    d. sitophobia

23. Change LOAF to FOOD in four steps, one letter at a time

    LOAF

    ――

    ――

    ――

    FOOD

24. What is the name given to a group of herons?

    a. brace

    b. colony

    c. covey

    d. knob

25. Find an eight-letter word. Each letter in the outer boxes is used once; the letters in the inner boxes are used twice.

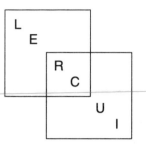

26. Find the weight to balance the scales.

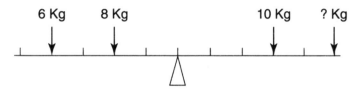

27. Move from letter to letter to find a seven-letter word; letters must be used only once.

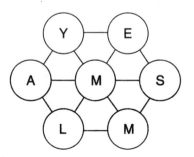

28. What single word is concealed in this anagram?

ITS IN CHARITY

29. Trace the chords across the circle and around the circumference to find a word.

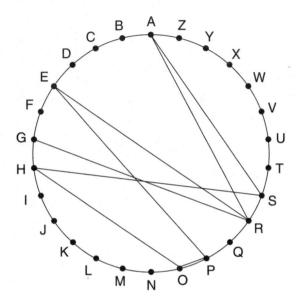

Clue: lawn jumper (11)

30. Which rectangle should replace the ?

A, B, C or D?

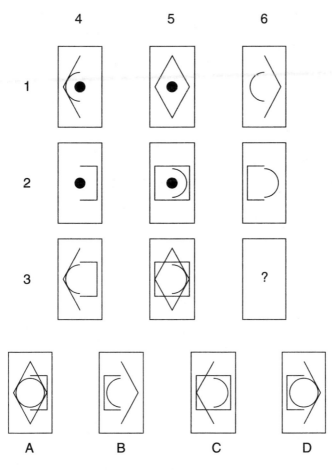

31. Which two words are antonyms?

conspicuous, unconcealed, diligence, enduring, pitiable, lavish, serenity, parsimonious

32. What is a synonym of PRECIPITOUS?

    guidance, contiguous, incessant, complaisance, evanescent, peaceful, sheer, infelicity

33. What do these words have in common?

    charming

    cleared

    chipped

    tulips

    cribbage

34. Find two animals of five letters out of these 10 letters.

    EHKKNRSSUW

35. Find the word, clockwise or anti-clockwise.
    Clue: a river.

36. Letters have been scrambled. Which group will not make a six-letter word?

    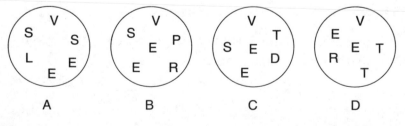

37. Solve the rebus.

IN
DEX

38. Find this trite saying by Groucho Marx.

A	AS	IT	IS
LIGHT	EAT	TO	IS
EATER	SHE	MY	AS
SOON	WIFE	STARTS	LIGHT

39. Find the highest scoring Scrabble word out of these tiles.

40. Which diamond should replace the ?

A, B, C or D?

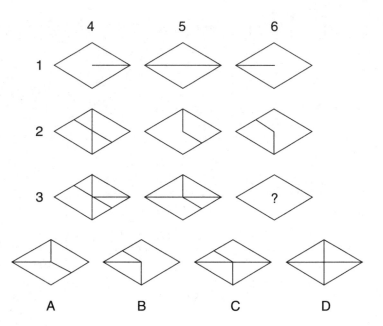

Test Three: Answers

1. B

2. peaceful, amicable

3. Fifty-six miles: seven days at 32 miles per day = 224. Walks on eighth day 40 miles = 264 to raise his average to 33 miles per day. If walks 56 miles on eighth day = 280, this would raise his average to 35 miles per day

4. b. market place

5. hornpipe; it is a folk dance, the rest are ballroom dances.

6. B; the diamond rotates 90 degrees and goes to the bottom, the square reduces in size and goes in the middle and the ellipse rotates 90 degrees and goes to the top. This reverses the analogy originally presented of figures in similar positions.

7. 7; $84/12 = 7 \; 14 \times 7 = 98$

8. paste, stick

9. donkey

10. A; the outer arc moves 90 degrees anti-clockwise, the middle arc moves 180 degrees and the inner arc moves 90 degrees clockwise.

11. 753/357; the rest are in pairs where each number in the top circle is repeated in the bottom circle with the last two digits reversed, for example 741/714; 753 and 357 have the first and last digits reversed.

12. E; it contains a triangle in a circle, a square in a triangle and a circle in a square.

13. AVENGE = Geneva; the dances are gavotte (vote tag), tango (Tonga), bolero (rob Leo) and minuet (tin emu).

14. E; in between the circles is a repeated sequence of shapes inverted the second time around.

15. 3; the sum of each column increases 1, 3, 5, 7 then decreases exactly the same on the other side.

16. bright eyed and bushy tailed

17. calculator

18. E; the right-hand side folds onto the left-hand side. The resultant figure then shrinks and goes inside the originally small figure in the top right-hand corner of the left figure.

19. 5; $4 \times 8 = 32$, $8 \times 7 = 56$, $3 \times 4 = 12$, therefore, $5 \times 9 = 45$

20. people

21. maroon

22. a. homichlophobia

23. LOAF, LOAD, GOAD, GOOD, FOOD

24. b. colony

25. curricle

26. 2 kg

27. malmsey

28. Christianity

29. grasshopper

30. D; 1 is added to 2 to equal 3, 4 is added to 5 to equal 6. Similar symbols disappear.

31. lavish, parsimonious

32. sheer

33. They all contain parts of the body.

    ARM, EAR, HIP, LIP, RIB

34. skunk, shrew

35. Missouri

36. D; A – VESSEL; B – VESPER; C – VESTED.

37. Index linked

38. My wife is a light eater; as soon as it is light she starts to eat.

39. jacket (19).

40. B; 1 is added to 2 to equal 3, 4 is added to 5 to equal 6 but similar symbols disappear.

Test Four: Questions

1. Which is the odd one out?

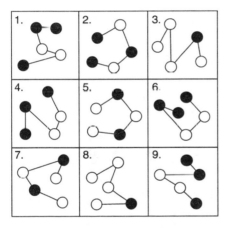

2. Solve the cryptic clue, two words (5, 8). The answer is an anagram contained within the clue.

PRICE REDUCTION NEGOTIATED FOR ODDEST CURTAIN

3. Which is the odd one out?

confront, condescend, adverse, polarize, oppugn

4. What number should replace the question mark?

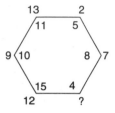

5. *Prunus domestica* is to plum as *Vitus vinifera* is to:
    cherry, prune, pomegranate, peach, grape.

6. What number continues the sequence?
    1, 10, 2.25, 8.25, 3.5, 6.5, 4.75, ?

7.

    What comes next in the above sequence?

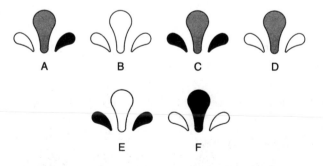

8. CROSS ANKLE is an anagram of which phrase (5, 5)?
    Clue: togetherness.

9.

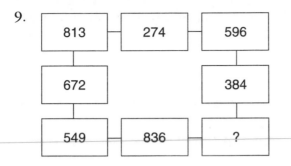

813	274	596
672		384
549	836	?

Which of the following numbers should replace the question mark?

417, 926, 138, 172 or 428

10.

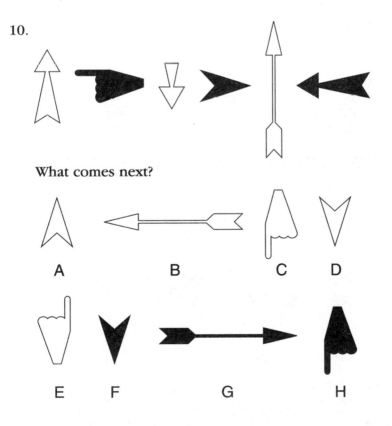

What comes next?

A   B   C   D

E   F   G   H

11. Change just one letter in each word to find a familiar phrase.

    MALE FOOD

12. What letter should replace the question mark?

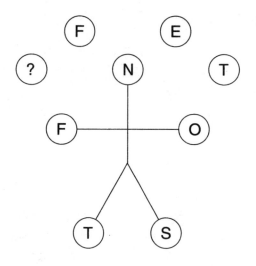

13. What number should replace the question mark?

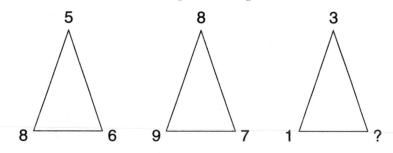

14.

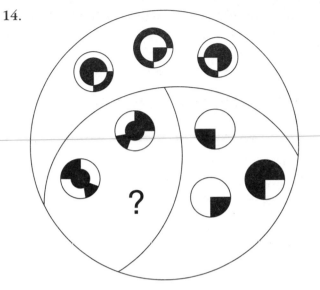

Which circle should replace the question mark?

A   B   C   D   E   F

15. Find two words that are antonyms. One word reads either clockwise or anti-clockwise around the outer circle and the other reads in the opposite direction in the inner circle. You must provide the missing letters.

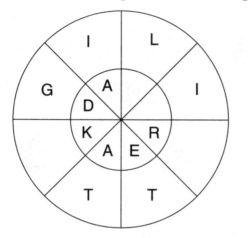

16. Which two words are closest in meaning?

cycle, hawk, convey, extort, peddle, summon

17.

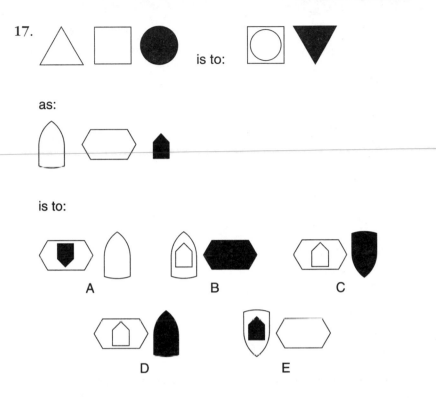

is to:

as:

is to:

18. Use each letter of the newspaper headline below once each only to spell out the names of three capital cities:

PRO-IMPERIAL RIOTS

19. What number should replace the question mark?

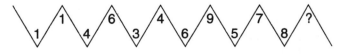

20.

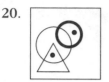

To which square below can a dot be added so that both dots then meet the same conditions as in the box above?

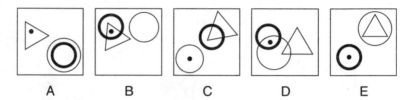

A   B   C   D   E

21. Find the word

– – – R O W F – –

(A type of pea.)

22. Find two heraldic terms of five letters out of these 10 letters.

A B E E G L L S S U

23. Find a one word anagram for

BITE METAL

24. What is a synonym for pragmatical?

conduce, cherished, becoming, deceptive, disquiet, adequate, conclusive, matter of fact

25. At the zoo, the numbers of the animals' cages were as follows:

    elephant 19

    seal 10

    monkey 14

    camel ?

    What was the camel's cage number?

26. How many different arrangements of the word PUZZLES can you make?

27. Place these nine items in three sets of three

    FISH – TREES – DRINK

    BLOATER ANISEED CURACAO KOUMISS REDWOOD

    POLLOCK POLYPUS DOGWOOD PERRIER

28. Find a one word anagram for

    HEED LARKS

29.

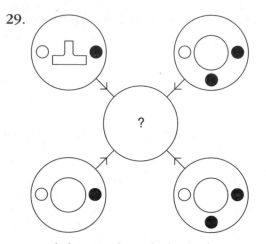

Each line and symbol which appears in the four outer circles, above, is transferred to the centre circle according to these rules. If a line or symbol occurs in the outer circles:

- once: it is transferred;
- twice: it is possibly transferred;
- three times: it is transferred;
- four times: it is not transferred.

Which of the circles A, B, C, D or E shown below should appear at the centre of the diagram, above?

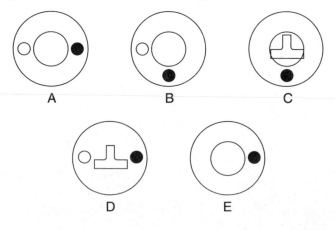

30. Find the highest scoring Scrabble word out of these tiles.

31. Place two four-letter bits together to equal a type of monument.

    TAPH EMPO MENS VICA RATE ABAT CENO RIUM
    MONU TOIS

32. What have these words in common?

    instructor, latest, encourage, pasteurized

33. Which two words are antonyms?

    whole, subvert, stirred, inspect, punish, repair, whit

34. Simplify and find value of x.

    $2 \times 7 \times 16 - (8 - 7) - (9 \div 3) = x$

35. Find seven animals in any direction but only in straight lines.

```
            H
        C   A   T
    L   U   T   E   T
T   E   R   E   V   E   L
    E   W   E   I   G
        O   H   C
        C
```

36. What is the name given to a group of hares?

    a. murmuration

    b. mute

    c. husk

    d. troop

    e. tiding

37. Fill in the blanks to find two words which are synonyms, clockwise or anti-clockwise.

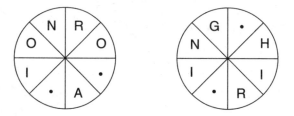

38. Move from letter to letter to find a seven-letter word. Each letter must be used only once.

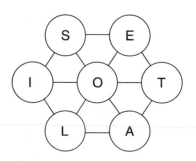

39. Find two words by moving across the circle on the chords, and along the circumference.

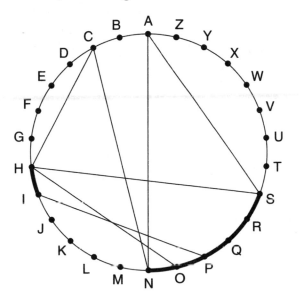

Clue: keeps the boat steady (5–6)

40. Each of the nine squares in the grid marked 1A to 3C should incorporate all the lines and symbols which are shown in the squares of the same letter and number immediately above and to the left. For example, 2B should incorporate all the lines and symbols that are in 2 and B. One of the squares is incorrect. Which one is it?

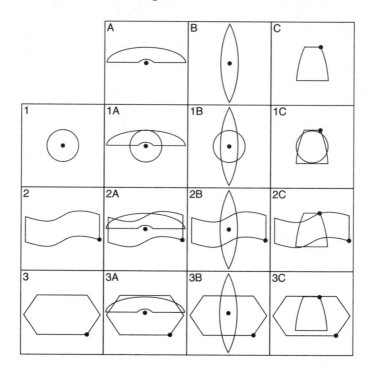

Test Four: Answers

1. 2; number 1 has the same chain as 6 (ie black/black/white/white/black), 3 has the same chain as 8, 4 has the same chain as 9, and 5 has the same chain as 7.

2. trade discount (oddest curtain).

3. condescend; it means agree, the rest meaning oppose.

4. 6; looking at alternate numbers appearing opposite each other the sum is the same, for example $13 + 4 = 11 + 6$ and $2 + 15 = 12 + 5$ etc.

5. grape

6. 4.75; there are two alternate sequences starting at 1 and 10 respectively. From 1 add 1.25 and from 10 deduct 1.75.

7. A; looking across, the large middle part alternates black, tinted, white, the left part alternates white, black and the right part alternates black, white.

8. close ranks

9. 172; so that each line contains the numbers 1–9 inclusive once each only.

10. C; there are five types of pointer that are repeated. At each stage the pointer rotates 90 degrees anti-clockwise, and the pointers alternate white/black.

11. make good

12. S; the letters being juggled with are the initials of the numbers One, Two, Three, Four, Five, Six, Seven, Eight, Nine.

13. 1; the numbers around the middle triangle are the sums of numbers in the same position around the end two tri-angles, for example 5 + 3 = 8.

14. E; in each segment there are two circles that are a mirror image of each other and two that have black/white rever-sal.

15. twilight, daybreak

16. peddle, hawk

17. C; the figure on the right changes from black to white and goes inside the figure in the middle. The figure on the left rotates 180 degrees and transfers to the right, also chang-ing from white to black.

18. Tripoli, Paris, Rome

19. 12; the top numbers proceed +5, −2 and the numbers at the bottom proceed +3, − 1.

20. E; so that one dot is in the small circle only and the other dot is in the large circle and triangle.

21. marrowfat

22. sable, gules

23. timetable

24. matter of fact

25. 12; consonant = 2, vowel = 3

26. 2520 $\dfrac{7!}{2}$ or $\dfrac{7 \times 6 \times 5 \times 4 \times 3 \times 2 \times 1}{2 \times 1}$

27. fish: bloater, pollock, polypus; trees: aniseed, redwood, dogwood; drink: curacao, koumiss, Perrier.

28. sheldrake

29. C

30. myrrh (13)

31. cenotaph

32. They all carry synonyms: TUTOR, LAST, URGE, PURE

33. whole, whit

34. $2 + 7 \times 16 - (8 - 7) - (9 \div 3) = x$

    $2 + (7 \times 16) - (8 - 7) - (9 \div 3) = x$

    $2 + 112 - 1 - 3 = 110$

35. cheetah, leveret, civet, cur, teg, ewe, cat

36. c. husk

37. rotation, whirling

38. isolate

39. ship's anchor

40. 1C

Test Five: Questions

1. SLY LOCATIONS is an anagram of which two words that are opposite in meaning?

2. Pentagon is to five as nonagon is to: seven, nine, 10, 12, 20.

3.

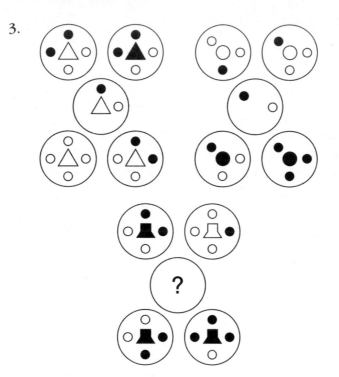

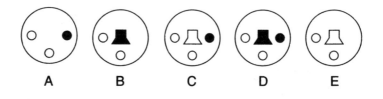

Which circle should replace the question mark?

A   B   C   D   E

4. T   S   R   A

    N   *   T   M

    I   L   O   *

Work from letter to adjacent letter horizontally and vertically (but not diagonally) to spell out a 12-letter word. You have to find the starting point and provide the missing letters.

5. Only one group of five letters below can be arranged to form a five-letter English word. Find the word.

OPLEB

ITDVA

GURAB

OUDCR

YABTO

6.

What comes next?

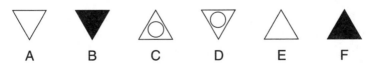

   A   B   C   D   E   F

7.   4863 – 2436

8132 – 4261

Which set of numbers below has the same relationship to each other as the sets of numbers above?

a. 5926 – 1813

b. 4621 – 2312

c. 9842 – 8421

d. 8346 – 4623

e. 6214 – 3122

8.   Solve the anagram in brackets to complete the quotation by Albert Einstein:

(COLLATING ECHO) progress is like an axe in the hands of a pathological criminal.

9.   100, 98.5, 95.5, 91, 85, ?

What number should replace the question mark?

10.

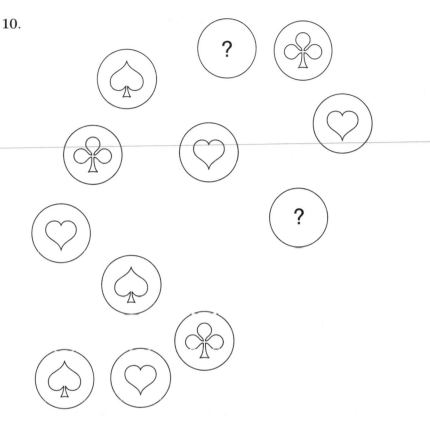

What should be contained in the two circles with the question marks?

11. What word means the same as the definitions either side of the brackets?

metal rod ( ) card game

12. Which two words are closest in meaning?

supreme, onerous, avaricious, exigent,
obscure, unsuitable

13. Which four of the five pieces below can be fitted together to form a perfect square?

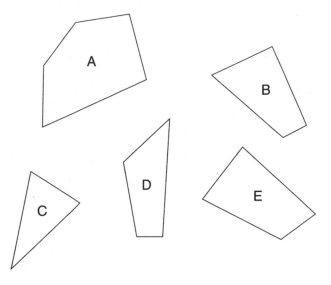

14. What number should replace the question mark?

	29				24				37	
43	32	21		39	31	23		58	?	28
	35				38				49	

15. Which is the odd one out?

warble, splutter, babble, prate, drawl

16. What number should replace the question mark?

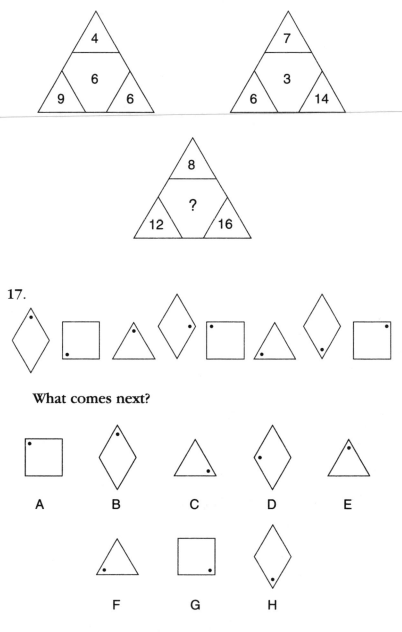

17.

What comes next?

18. Find two words which are antonyms. One word reads either clockwise or anti-clockwise round the outer circle and the other reads in the opposite direction in the inner circle. You must provide the missing letters.

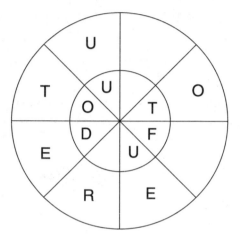

19. What number should replace the question mark?

		3				
					9	
15			?			21
	27			24		
					34	
		40				36
			46			

20.

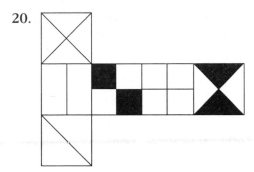

When the above is folded to form a cube, which is the only one of the following that can be produced?

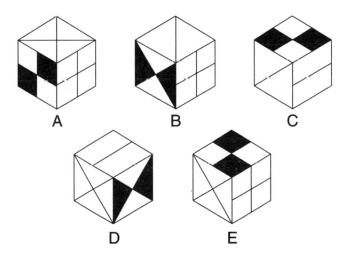

21. Which two words mean the opposite?

incarcerate, sly, artifice, shrewd, inflame, incense, release, robust

22. Replace the letters in the blanks to find 3 kitchen utensils.

    –H–N–W–R–

    –O–R–N–E–

    –I–E–L–S–

23. Place two three-letters bits together to equal a MUSICAL INSTRUMENT.

    SPI DLE TIM HEN LEN

    BEL VIO NIT ZIT FID

24. If 48 = 60, what does 27 = ?

25. Find a nine-letter word in any direction; each letter can only be used once.

S	A	M	U
R	G	H	W
B	L	I	T
O	N	E	C

26. Fill in the blanks to find two words that are synonyms, clockwise or anti-clockwise.

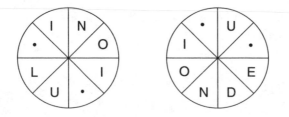

27. The combined age of Alan and Bill is 86. The combined age of Bill and Claude is 73. The combined age of Alan and Claude is 15. How old are:

    Alan?

    Bill?

    Claude?

28. Find the 12-letter word.

T E C	R A S	M N O
S E G	P W N Q	R D T
O X F	D Y R	C H E

29. Which hexagon should replace the ?

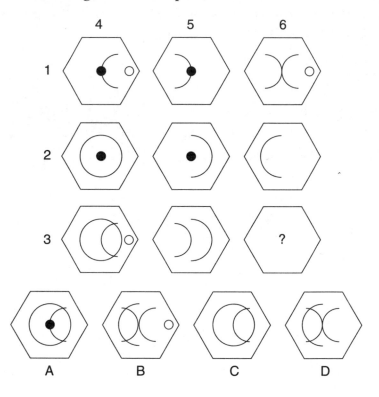

30. Each of the nine squares in the grid marked 1A to 3C, should incorporate all the lines and symbols that are shown in the squares of the same letter and number immediately above and to the left. For example, 2B should incorporate all the lines and symbols that are in 2 and B.

One of the squares is incorrect. Which one is it?

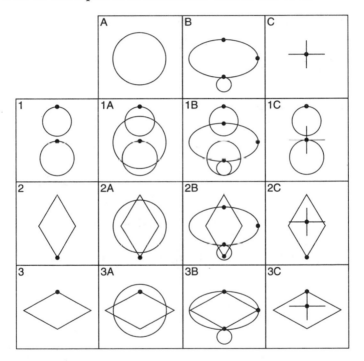

31. Find a six-letter word out of these four letters, using two of the letters twice: T E F R.

32. Find two MINERALS of five letters out of these 10 letters.

A A E E H L L S S T

33. What have these words in common?

    fatigue

    exhilaration

    deliberate

    hurries

34. Which two words mean the same?

    rectitude, nefarious, essential, importunity, manifest, ridicule, honesty, assertion

35. Find the weight to balance the scales.

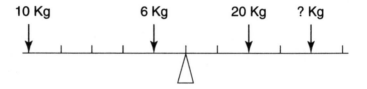

36. Find this humorous saying by Groucho Marx.

ON	MADE	EXCHANGE	A
MY	THE	BROKER	SHOT
KILLING	I	I	STOCK

37. Find a seven-letter word by moving from letter to letter; each letter must only be used once.

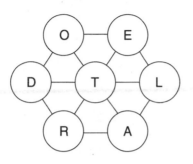

38. The letters in the circles below have been scrambled. Which circle will not make a six-letter word?

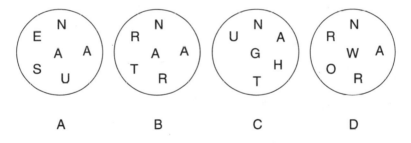

A   B   C   D

39. Find two words by moving across the circle on the chords, and along the circumference.

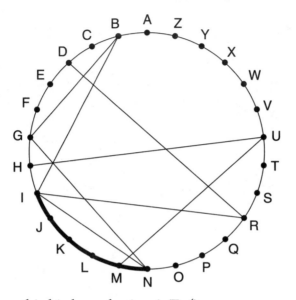

Clue: this bird nearly sings! (7–4)

40. Each of the nine squares marked 1A to 3C in the grid should incorporate all the lines and symbols that are shown in the squares of the same letter and number immediately above and to the left. For example, 2B should incorporate all the lines and symbols that are in 2 and B. One of the squares is incorrect. Which one is it?

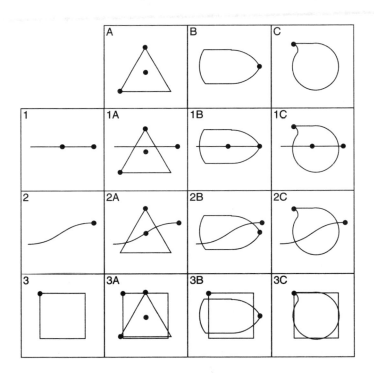

Test Five: Answers

1. tiny, colossal

2. nine

3. B; only when a symbol appears three times in the same position in the outer circles is it transferred to the middle circle.

4. trampolinist

5. ITDVA = davit

6. D; every third triangle is inverted, every fifth triangle is black, every fourth triangle has a dot in it.

7. d. 8346 – 4623; every even number is halved and every odd number is doubled.

8. technological

9. 77.5; the amount deducted increases by 1.5 each time, ie 1.5, 3, 4.5, 6, 7.5.

10. Spade at the top and club in the lower circle: starting at the bottom spade and snaking upwards each group of three circles contains a spade, a heart and a club.

11. poker

12. onerous, exigent

13.

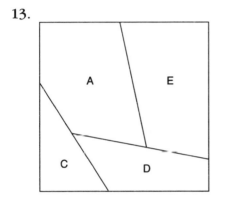

14. 43; the number in the middle is half the sum of the numbers either side and top and bottom.

15. warble ; it is a type of song, the rest being types of speech.

16. 6; $8 \times 12 = 96 \div 16 = 6$

17. C; there are three figures, diamond, square and triangle being repeated. In the diamond and square the dot is moving one corner clockwise at each stage, but in the triangle it is moving one corner anti-clockwise.

18. resolute, doubtful

19. 18; start at the top left-hand square and work along the top row, then back along the second row etc. The numbers represent the number of squares counting from the top left-hand square.

20. D

21. incarcerate, release

22. chinaware, porringer, wineglass

23. fiddle

24. 33 in Modular 8, 48 Mod 10 = 60 Mod 8, 27 Mod 10 = 33 Mod 8.

25. lethargic

26. illusion, delusion

27. Alan 14, Bill 72, Claude 1.

28. fostermother (around outside)

29. B; 1 is added to 2 to equal 3, 4 is added to 5 to equal 6, but similar symbols disappear.

30. 1B

31. ferret

32. slate, shale

33. They all contain synonyms: FAG, ELATION, DEBATE, HIES

34. rectitude, honesty

35. 4 kg   10 kg × 5 = 50 kg   20 kg × 2 = 40 kg
                  6 kg × 1 = 6 kg   4 kg × 4 = 16 kg
                  ———————————   ———————————
                             56 kg   56 kg

36. I made a killing on the stock exchange. I shot my broker.

37. leotard

38. B

    A: NAUSEA

    C: NAUGHT

    D: NARROW

39. humming bird

40. 1A

Test Six: Questions

1. Sunday

   Monday

   Tuesday

   Wednesday

   Thursday

   Friday

   Saturday

   What day comes immediately after the day that comes three days before the day that comes two days before the day that comes immediately after the day that comes two days after Wednesday?

2. Only one group of five letters below can be arranged to form a five-letter English word. Find the word.

   EDBIL

   NUREF

   LORDA

   BURAM

   FEDCO

3.

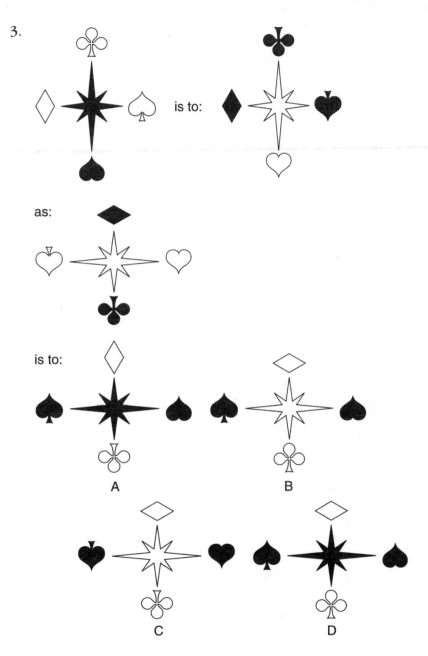

A

B

C

D

4. 4 5 6 3 3 6

    7 2 3 4 7

    5 8 2 4

    7 2 6

    8 3

    ?

    What number should replace the question mark?

5. What letter should replace the question mark?

C	C	R		I	N	T		I	S	N
S	H	I		E	S	T		I	A	?

6. Peridot is to green as moonstone is to: violet, blue, yellow, red, white.

7. What number should replace the question mark?

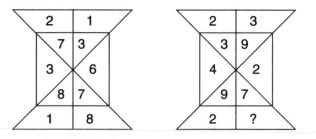

8.

What comes next?

A   B   C   D   E

9. GIANT CAMEL is an anagram of which 10-letter word?

10. Which four of the five pieces below can be fitted together to form a perfect square?

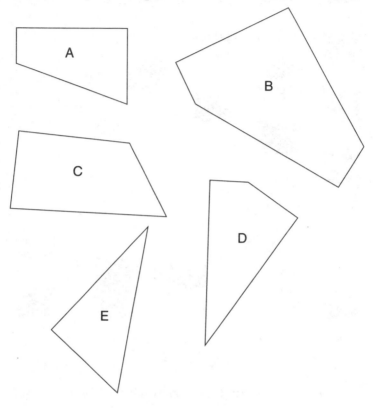

11. A manufacturer wishes to offer his customer a discount of 25 per cent and make 12.5 cent profit over and above his cost price. If his cost price is £32, what should be his gross selling price (ie before discount) in order to achieve the required profit margin?

12. What word means the same as the definitions outside the brackets?

ceremonial staff ( ) type of spice

13. Which two words are most opposite in meaning?

    cowardice, bigotry, bias, tolerance, modesty, tenacity

14. Which is the odd one out?

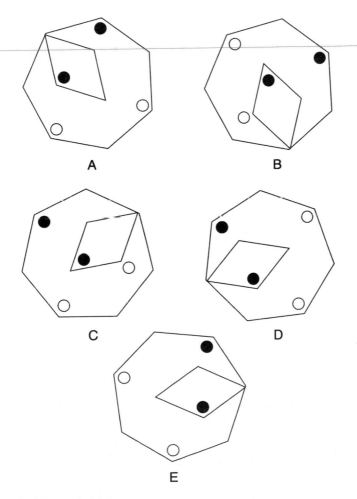

15. Which is the odd one out?

    orange, purple, yellow, blue, lemon

16. What numbers should appear on the bottom line?

     12   7   9

     21 19 16

     37 40 35

     72 77 75

      ?   ?   ?

17. 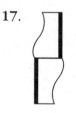   is to:

    as:

    is to:

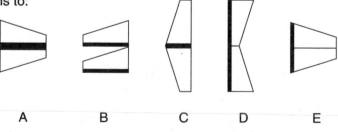

    A   B   C   D   E

18. Find two words which are synonyms. One word reads either clockwise or anti-clockwise round the outer circle and the other reads in the opposite direction in the inner circle. You must provide the missing letters.

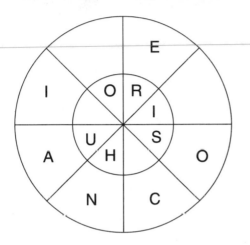

19. 3412, 4223, 2334, 3442, ?

What number comes next?

20.

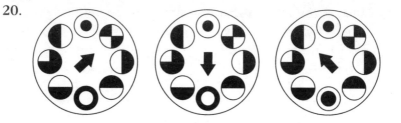

What comes next?

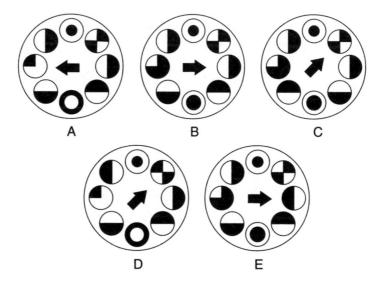

21. Find a six-letter word out of these four letters, using two of the letters twice: D, E, W, B.

22. Place two four-letter bits together to form a POISON.

   LISN PHOS ANTI AINE PARA

   QUAR MONI PTOM GINE BOTO

23. What is the name given to a group of arrows?

    a. pattern

    b. battery

    c. flight

    d. quiver

24. Which two words mean the opposite?

    invariable, admissable, resolved, beset, incipient, ending, baleful, sufferance

25. How many revolutions must the largest cog make in order to bring the cogs back to their original positions?

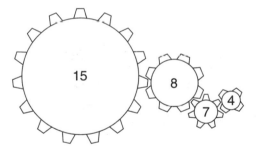

26. In the cross country race:

    ● Brown came in 22nd;

    ● Williams came in 31st;

    ● Jones came in 19th;

    ● Samuels came in ?

    What position was Samuels?

27. Place the nine items in three sets of three.

   FOOD – SHIPS – REPTILES

   brisket

   compote

   monitor

   carrack

   snapper

   clipper

   dariole

   collier

   saurian

28. Find a six-letter word made up of five letters.

E	M	T
X	S	B
E	C	T

29. Which number is the odd one out?

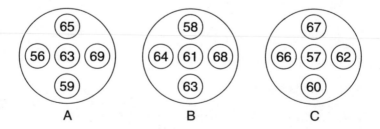

A   B   C

30. Find the highest scoring SCRABBLE word out of these tiles.

31. Simplify and find the value of x.

    $6 + 2 \times 4 - 6 \div 2 - 4 - (2 \times 10) + 6 = x$

32. Find two five-letter BOATS out of these 10 letters.

    A A E F K K R R Y Y

33. What do these words have in common?

    speared

    sublime

    undated

    engaged

    shipped

34. Which two words mean the same?

    infamous, uncandid, redolent, discern, incorporeal, insidious, dissociate, fragrant

35. Which seven-letter word is contained in the circles below.

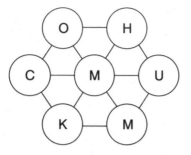

36. Which is an anagram that will not spell out a COLOUR?

    a. SAFFROS

    b. COTIRAP

    c. MIRECAN

    d. MISCRNO

37. Solve the REBUS.

    TOCCDUN

38. Find six BIRDS in any direction but only in straight lines.

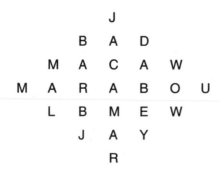

39. Find two words by moving across the circle on the chords, and along the circumference.

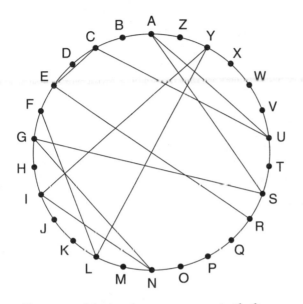

Clue: trouble in the restaurant! (6–6)

40. Which oval should replace the ?

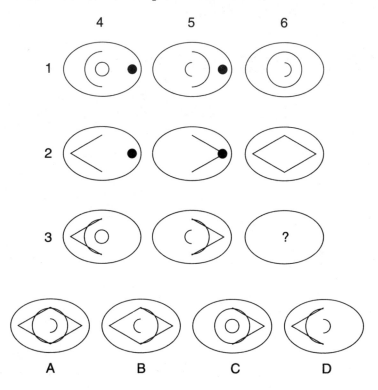

Test Six: Answers

1. Tuesday

2. BURAM = umbra or rumba

3. D; each symbol rotates 180 degrees and changes from black to white or vice versa.

4. 7; the sums of numbers in lines across reduce by four each time – ie 27, 23, 19, 15, 11, 7.

5. T; follow the route shown below to spell out the two words Christian Scientist.

C	C	R	I	N	T	I	S	N
S	H	I	E	S	T	I	A	T

6. white

7. 8; $23 \times 4 = 92$ and $39 \times 2 = 78$

8. E; take out the third link from the top each time

9. magnetical

10.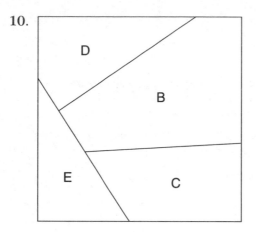

11. £48: 32 + 12.5% = 36 + 1/3 = 48

12. mace

13. bigotry, tolerance

14. E; A is the same as D and B is the same as C.

15. lemon; the rest are all colours of the spectrum.

16.

147	149	152
A	B	C
12	7	9
21	19	16
A + C = A	A + B = B	B + C = C

17. B; the top figure flips over horizontally and the bottom figure flips over vertically.

18. humorist, comedian

19. 4253; each number swaps round as follows – A B C D (3 4 1 2) to B D C A (4 2 2 3), and so on. However, the third number, whilst remaining in the same position each time, increases by one at each stage.

20. B; the arrow moves three circles clockwise at each stage. After it has pointed to a circle, that circle reverses black and white sections at subsequent stages.

21. webbed

22. ptomaine

23. d. quiver

24. incipient, ending

25. 56

26. 26; consonants 5, vowels 2.

27. food: brisket, compote, dariole. ships: carrack, clipper, collier. reptiles: monitor, snapper, saurian.

28.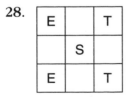

29. 63; there are two 63s.

30. chick (16)

31. Orders must be taken ( ), $\times$, $\div$, $+$, $-$

    $6 + 2 \times 4 - 6 \div 2 - 4 - (2 \times 10) + 6 = x$

    $6 + (2 \times 4) - (6 \div 2) - 4 - (2 \times 10) + 6 = x$

    $6 + \quad 8 \quad - \quad 3 \quad - 4 - \quad 20 \quad + 6 = -7$

32. ferry, kayak

33. They all contain fruit

    pear, lime, date, gage, hip

34. redolent, fragrant

35. hummock

36. a. saffros (b. apricot c. carmine d. crimson)

37. disorderly conduct

38. jacamar, marabou, macaw, barb, jay, mew

39. flying saucer

40. A; 1 is added to 2 to equal 3; 4 is added to 5 to equal 6, but similar symbols disappear.

Test Seven: Questions

1. Which is the odd one out?

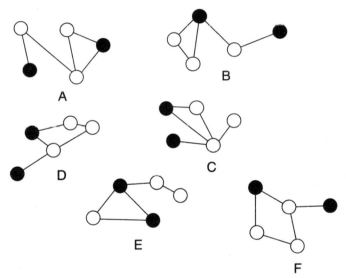

2. Cardiology is to heart as renology is to: chest, kidney, nose, nerves, brain.

3. Mary has a third as many again as Mike who has a third again as Molly. In total they have 148. How many has each?

4. Complete the six words so that the same two letters that finish the first word start the second word and the same two letters that finish the second word start the third word, and so on. The same two letters that finish the sixth word also start the first word, to complete the circle.

    – –AM – –

    – – AP – –

    – – AR – –

    – – AN – –

    – – LL – –

    – – IS – –

5. Which word in brackets is opposite in meaning to the word in capitals?

    SCURRILOUS
    (civilized, dishonest, neat, unhurried, sensible)

6.

8	1	2	9
6	3	5	7
2	3	7	1
3	1	8	9

9	1	1	7
2	8	7	5
8	9	3	6
1	3	2	3

Which four digits appear in the same order in a straight line in both grids? The digits can appear horizontally, vertically or diagonally, backwards or forwards.

7.

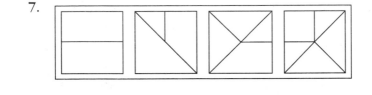

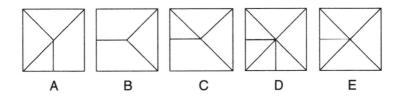

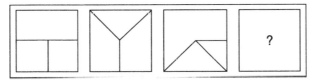

What should replace the question mark?

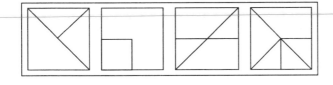

A　　　　B　　　　C　　　　D　　　　E

8. If presented with the words MAR, AM and FAR and asked to find the shortest word that contained all the letters from which these words could be produced you should come up with the word FARM.

Here is a further list of words:

ROMANCE ACRONYM EDUCATE

What is the shortest English word from which all these words can be produced?

9. Which is the odd one out?

    prairie, pampas, massif, savannah, veld

10. How many minutes is it before 12 noon if 90 minutes ago it was four times as many minutes past 9 am?

11.

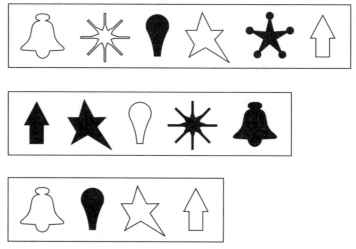

What comes next?

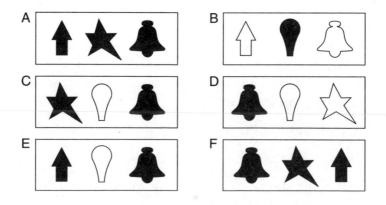

12. SORRIER ANIMAL is an anagram of which two words that are similar in meaning?

13.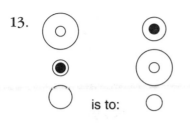

      is to:

as: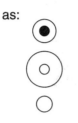

is to:

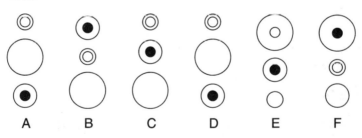

   A   B   C   D   E   F

14.

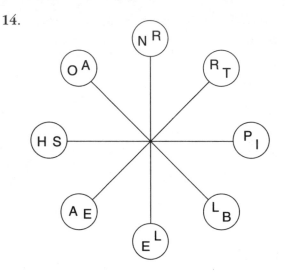

Take one letter from each circle in turn and reading clockwise find two words that are antonyms. All letters are used once each only and each word starts at a different circle.

15. Which of the following is not an anagram of a type of work or profession?

OIL ART

BAR KEN

COD ROT

COPY MAN

MR FEAR

16.

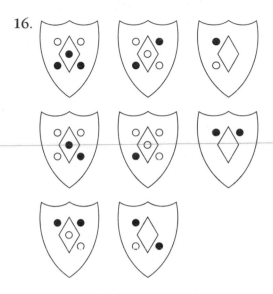

Which is the missing shield?

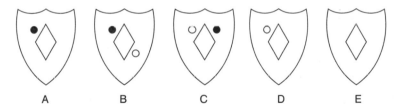

A   B   C   D   E

17. 73695287653196482

Multiply the number of even numbers in the above list
that are immediately followed by an odd number, by the
number of odd numbers that are immediately followed
by an even number.

18. What is the longest English word that can be produced
from the following 10 letters?

MIANTLTRPO

19.

45	16	9	11	15	32
21	61	28	27	12	1
65	8	55	19	7	56
24	13	2	25	14	5
62	67	30	10	29	59
3	6	17	12	4	18

What number is two places away from itself plus three, one place away from itself plus five, three places away from itself less one, two places away from itself plus two and three places away from itself less four?

20. Which is the odd one out?

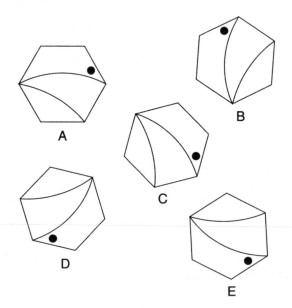

21. Which two words are synonyms?

    address, polite, heedless, animated, impulsive, homily, inane, trenchant

22. Simplify

    $$\frac{7}{13} \div \frac{28}{52} = x$$

23. How many different arrangements can you make from the word ARRANGE?

24. What is an antonym of alterable?

    irrevocable, capacious, sensual, calumny, emaciated, lassitude, lustful, prurient

25. Find the weight to balance the scales.

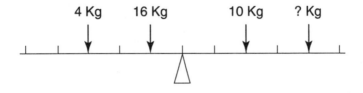

26. Fill in the blanks to find two words which are antonyms, clockwise or anti-clockwise.

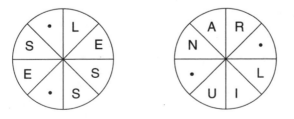

27. Find a nine-letter word by moving from letter to letter in any direction.

    Each letter can only be used once.

D	Y	W	E
M	R	L	C
A	V	O	F
B	G	F	N

28. Sort out this trite saying.

MAP	TO	YOU
EXCEPT	EVERYTHING	ROAD
TELLS	FOLD	IT
HOW	A	ALWAYS

29. What number should replace the ?

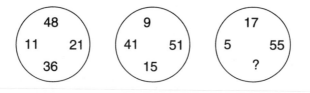

30.

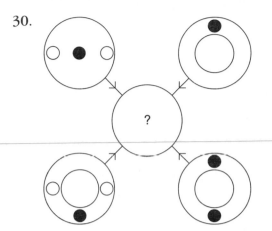

Each line and symbol that appears in the four outer circles above is transferred to the centre circle according to these rules. If a line or symbol occurs in the outer circles:

- once: it is transferred;
- twice: it is possibly transferred;
- three times: it is transferred;
- four times: it is not transferred.

Which of the circles A, B, C, D or E shown below should appear at the centre of the diagram, above?

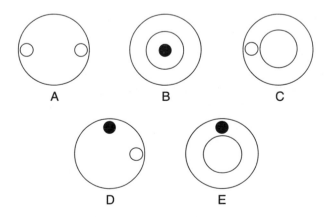

31. What is the fear of empty rooms?

    a. ideophobia

    b. dipsophobia

    c. pantaphobia

    d. kenophobia

32. Solve the following one-word anagram:

    DOOR BELL

33. Place two three-letter bits together to equal a geographical term.

    SIE ENE LEI HAM PAM

    VAL PAS LES RAV RRE

34. What do these words have in common?

    gusto

    becalmed

    tawdry

    cheated

    policy

35. Solve the following one-word anagram:

    SOME GREAT

36. Find the trite saying and its author.

WELL	WHY	WRONG	I
ANSWER	CALLED	THURBER	DID
NUMBER	IF	PHONE	THE
YOU	JAMES	THE	?

37. Move from letter to letter to spell out a 10-letter word. Each word may only be used once.

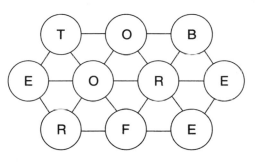

38. Make a nine-letter word out of this grid using all nine letters in the grid.

E	F	D
R	E	N
D	S	E

39. Find a word by moving across the circle on the chords, and along the circumferemce.

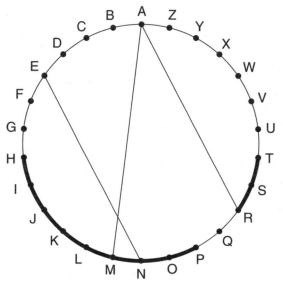

Clue: exercise for a down and out! (10)

40.

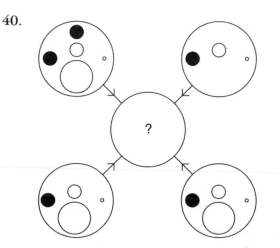

Each line and symbol that appears in the four outer

circles above, is transferred to the centre circle according to these rules. If a line or symbol occurs in the outer circles:

- once: it is transferred;
- twice: it is possibly transferred;
- three times: it is transferred;
- four times: it is not transferred.

Which of the circles A, B, C, D or E shown below should appear at the centre of the diagram, opposite?

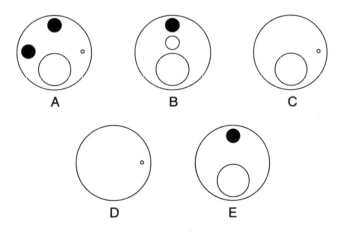

A   B   C

D   E

Test Seven: Answers

1. E; it is the only one in which the two black dots are directly connected

2. kidney

3. Molly 36, Mike 48, Mary 64.

4. enamel, elapse, search, chance, cellar, arisen

5. civilized

6. 1732

7. C; in each line one of the squares contains all the lines appearing in the other squares, with the exception of lines that appear in the other squares more than once. In line one it is the third square, in line two it is the second square and in line three it is the fourth square (option C).

8. documentary

9. massif; it is a highland region, the rest are grassland.

10. 18 minutes

11. E; each line reverses the line above and discards the symbol next to the end, also all symbols change from black to white and vice versa at each stage.

12. sailor, mariner

13. C; the circle at the bottom moves to the top, the circle at the top moves to the middle and the circle in the middle moves to the bottom. The dot in the middle circle moves to the circle at the top.

14. horrible, pleasant

15. COPY MAN = company

The jobs are tailor (oil art), banker (bar Ken), doctor (cod rot) and farmer (Mr Fear).

16. D; in each line across and down, only circles common to the first two shields are carried forward to the third shield; however, two white circles become a black circle and vice versa.

17. 12

18. important

19. 8

20. E; all the rest are the same figure rotated

21. homily, address

22. $\dfrac{7}{13} \div \dfrac{28}{52}$

$= \dfrac{7}{13} \times \dfrac{52}{28} = \dfrac{7}{13} \times \dfrac{4}{4} = \dfrac{4}{4} = 1$

23. $1260 = \dfrac{7!}{2 \times 2} = \dfrac{7 \times 6 \times 5 \times 4 \times 3 \times 2 \times 1}{2 \times 2}$

24. irrevocable

25. 2kg

4kg × 3 = 12kg	10kg × 2 = 20kg
16kg × 1 = 16kg	2kg × 4 = 8kg
28kg	28kg

26. restless, tranquil

27. dragonfly

28. A road map always tells you everything except how to fold it.

29. 3; Add digits in each circle = 26.

30. B

31. d. kenophobia

32. bordello

33. pampas

34. They all contain words to do with the weather GUST, CALM, DRY, HEAT, ICY.

35. gasometer

36. Well if I called the wrong number why did you answer the phone? James Thurber.

37. freebooter

38. defenders

39. trampoline

40. E

Test Eight: Questions

1. Which is the odd one out?

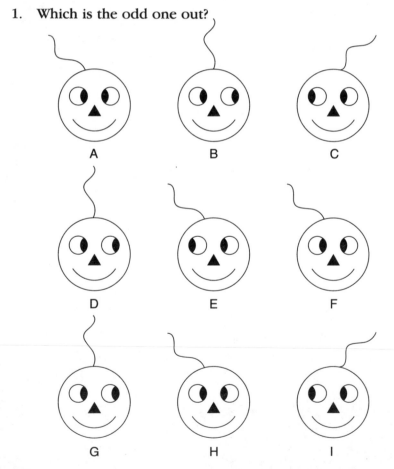

A

B

C

D

E

F

G

H

I

2. Solve the clues to find four six-letter words. The same three letters are represented by **XYZ** in each word.

   XYZ*** accounts book

   *XYZ** undertaking

   **XYZ* city in Spain

   ***XYZ cried loudly

3. What number should replace the question mark?

   4936: 67

   2581: 95

   1664: ?

4. Which word, when placed in the brackets, completes the first word and starts the second?

   REACT ( ) BIT

5. Solve the anagram in brackets to complete the quotation by Fred Allen.

   (GARDEN VISIT) is 85 per cent confusion and 15 per cent commission.

6. Which number should replace the question mark?

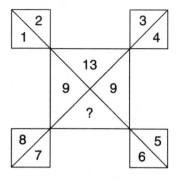

7.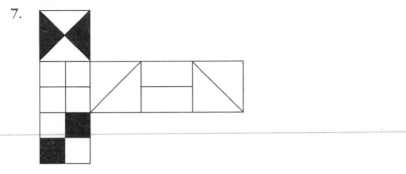

When the above is folded to form a cube, which is the only one of the following that can be produced?

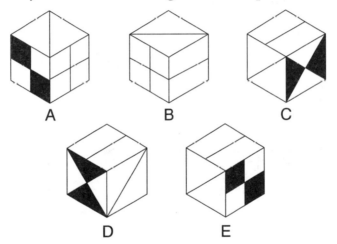

8. ABCDEFGH

Which letter is two to the left of the letter immediately to the right of the letter that is three to the right of the letter immediately to the left of the letter D?

9. What number should replace the question mark?

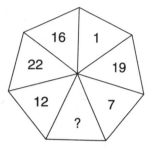

10.

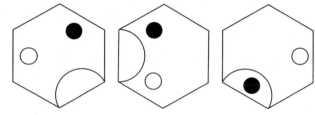

What comes next?

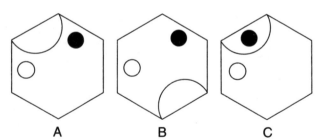

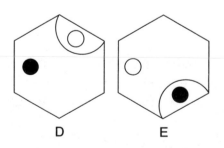

11.

23	6	14	2	15
4	12	25	8	16
10	18	1	5	22
11	24	7	20	3
17	19	13	21	1

Change the position of three numbers only to form a magic number square where each horizontal, vertical and corner to corner line adds up to 65.

12. Which two words are most opposite in meaning?

waspish, tenuous, free, wayward, bleak, genial

13.

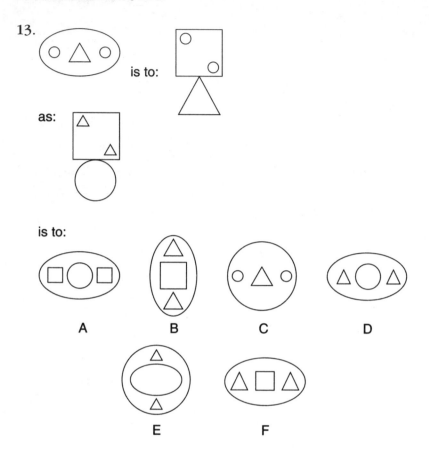

14. Sally has half as many again as Sue who has half as many again as Sam. Together they have 152. How many has each?

15. Barometer is to atmospheric pressure as odometer is to: distance, ductility, voltage, time, speed.

16. Which is the odd one out?

    ram, lion, pig, goat, bull

17.

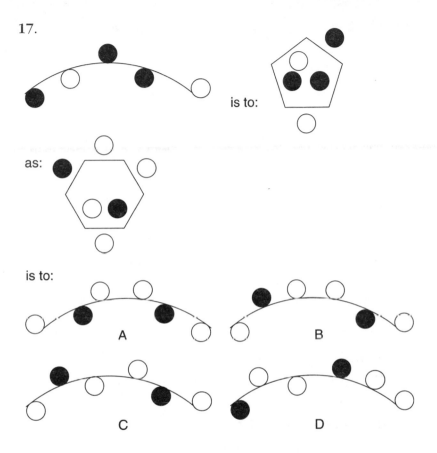

18. Which of the following is not an anagram of a musical instrument?

NO CERT

BOON ASS

TUG AIR

COP COIL

RED BAG

19. Which word in brackets is closest in meaning to the word in capitals?

    ELUCIDATE
    (adorn, articulate, pronounce, dodge, interpret)

20.

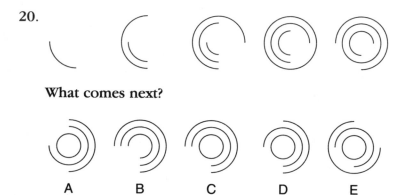

    What comes next?

    A   B   C   D   E

21. Simplify
    $$\frac{83}{27} \div \frac{166}{9} = x$$

22. Simplify, find value of x.

    $4 - 17 \times 2 + 90 \div 6 - 7 = x$

23. Place two four-letter bits together to make a TREE.

    SYCA RISS OLEA CALA HAWT

    HORN MAGN PASH NORE TAMA

24. Which two words are synonyms?

    inculcate, apprehend, gratify, celebrate, unsullied, possible, infuse, aspect

25. How many revolutions must the largest cog make in order to bring the cogs back to their original positions?

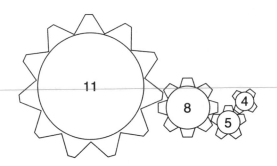

26. Which anagram will not spell out a BOY'S NAME?

    a. RATHOOI

    b. NETHNEK

    c. NEALROD

    d. DERBICK

27. Move from letter to letter to spell out a 10 letter word, each letter may only be used once.

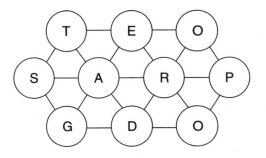

28. Solve the REBUS

29. Each of the nine squares in the grid marked 1A to 3C should incorporate all the lines and symbols that are shown in the squares of the same letter and number immediately above and to the left. For example, 2B should incorporate all the lines and symbols that are in 2 and B. One of the squares is incorrect. Which one is it?

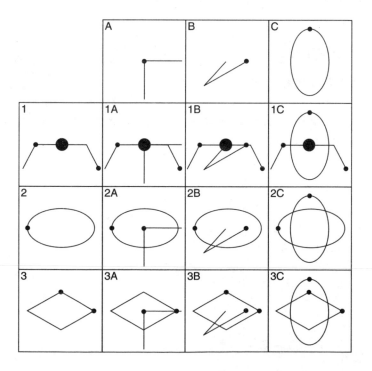

30. Which hexagon should replace the ? A, B, C or D?

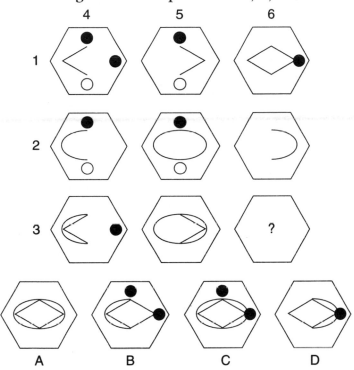

31. What is an antonym of ERUDITION?

   ignorance, occasion, exhilarated, appropriate, faithful, trustful, indolent, dullness

32. Replace the letters in the blanks to find three weather terms.

   – R – Z – L – N –

   – A – N – L – U –

   – I – H – N – N –

33. Find a six-letter word out of these four letters.

    NE

    TJ

34. What have these words in common?

    facetiousness

    masculine

    evacuate

    chocolate

35. Find six FISH in any direction but only in straight lines.

```
            G
        C   O   D
    K   R   U   A   E
G   O   U   R   N   E   T
    C   F   A   U   L
        F   M   T
            I
```

36. How may different arrangements can you make of the word CARACAS?

37. Fill in the blanks to find two words that are antonyms.

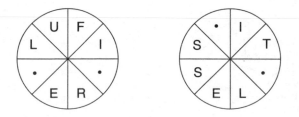

38. In the bird house, the cages were numbered:

    parrots 17

    eagles 12

    penguins 18

    vultures ?

    What was the cage number of the vultures?

39. Which circle should replace the ?

    A, B, C or D?

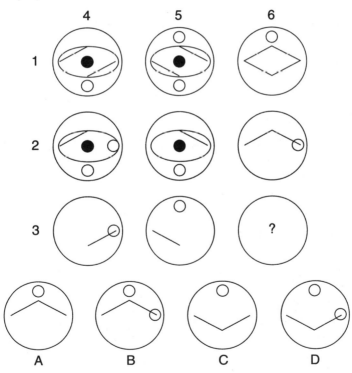

40. Find a word by moving across the circle on the chords and along the circumference.

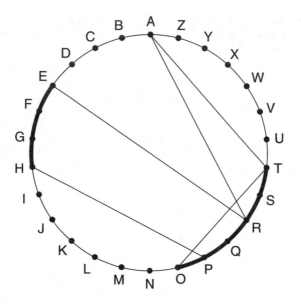

Clue: you don't go much higher (12)

Test Eight: Answers

1. E; in all the others eyes left is curl right. The rule is squint = curl left, eyes right = curl straight up, eyes left = curl right.

2. XYZ = LED; ledger, pledge, Toledo, howled

3. 48; the first digit of the second number is the square root of the last two digits of the first number and the second digit of the second number is the square root of the first two digits of the first number.

4. or, to make 'reactor' and 'orbit'.

5. advertising

6. 5; each group of three numbers, positioned north, south, east and west totals 18; ie 2 + 13 + 3 = 18.

7. C

8. E

9. 21; start at 1 and jumping two segments clockwise each time add 6, 5, 4, 3, 2, 1.

10. A; the black circle moves one side, then two, then three sides anti-clockwise; the arc moves two clockwise, one anti-clockwise, two clockwise etc; and the white circle one side, then two, then three sides anti-clockwise.

11.

23	6	19	2	15
4	12	25	8	16
10	18	1	14	22
11	24	7	20	3
17	5	13	21	1

12. waspish, genial

13. D; the square becomes an ellipse, the circle reduces in size and goes in the middle of the ellipse, and the triangles go either side of the circle in the ellipse; thus reversing the analogy of figures in similar positions in the original.

14. Sam 32, Sue 48, Sally 72.

15. distance

16. pig; pig is an animal in Chinese astrology; the rest are animals connected with signs of the Zodiac.

17. B; the hexagon becomes a curve. Circles inside the hexagon go below the curve and circles outside the hexagon above the curve, in the same order starting with the white circle inside the hexagon on the left and working clockwise.

18. RED BAG = badger. The musical instruments are cornet (no cert), bassoon (boon ass), guitar (tug air) and piccolo (cop coil).

19. interpret

20. D; the three circles are being constructed an arc at a time working clockwise, but once constructed disappear an arc at a time, also clockwise.

21. $\dfrac{83}{27} \div \dfrac{166}{9} = \dfrac{83}{27} \times \dfrac{9}{166} = \dfrac{3}{2} = 1\frac{1}{2}$

22. Order must be taken ( ), $\times$, $\div$, $+$, $-$

    $4 - (17 \times 2) + (90 \div 6) - 7 = x$

    $4 - \quad 34 \quad + \quad 15 \quad - 7 = -22$

23. hawthorn

24. inculcate, infuse

25. 40

26. d. DERBRICK

    a. HORATIO

    b. KENNETH

    c. LEONARD

27. gasteropod

28. A square meal

29. 3A

30. D; 1 is added to 2 to equal 3, 4 is added to 5 to equal 6, but similar symbols disappear.

31. erudition, ignorance

32. drizzling, raincloud, lightning

33. jennet

34. They all contain synonyms: FUN, MALE, VACATE, COCOA

35. GOURAMI, RUFF, COD, GOURNET, TUNA, EEL

36. $840 = \dfrac{7!}{3 \times 2} = \dfrac{7 \times 6 \times 5 \times 4 \times 3 \times 2 \times 1}{3 \times 2}$

37. merciful, pityless

38. 18; consonants = 3, vowels = 1.

39. D; 1 is added to 2 to equal 3, 4 is added to 5 to equal 6, but similar symbols disappear.

40. stratosphere

Test Nine: Questions

1. How many lines appear below?

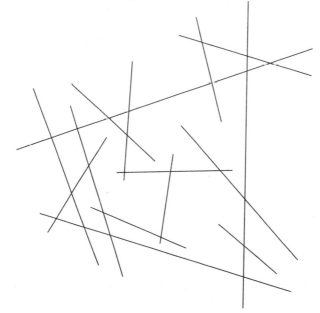

2. ALLEGED ARTIFICE is an anagram of which two words that are similar in meaning?

3. What number should replace the question mark?

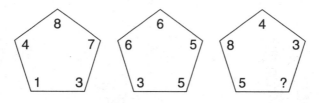

4. What letter should replace the question mark?

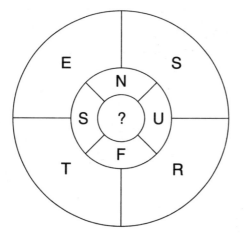

5. Which is the odd one out?

furlough, fanlight, realtor, diaper, sophomore

6. Which is the odd one out?

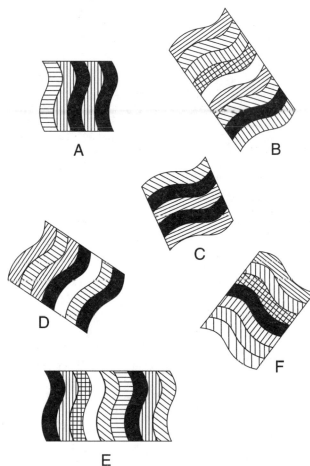

7. Which word in brackets is most opposite in meaning to the word in capitals?

IRREGULAR (apposite, steady, logical, careful, pious)

8.   7, 4, 11, 2, 14, 5, 18, 3, 21, ?

What comes next?

9.

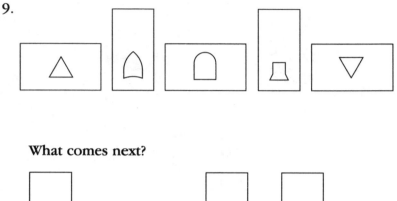

What comes next?

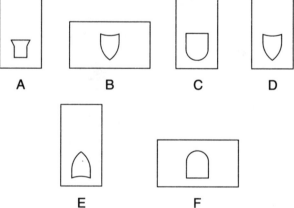

10. What is the longest English word that can be produced from the following 10 letters?

ALDUOINBTK

11. Strut is to swagger as sashay is to: saunter, trudge, slink, ramble, hobble.

12. Which number is the odd one out?

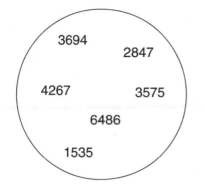

13.

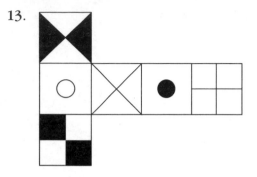

When the above is folded to form a cube, which is the only one of the following that can be produced?

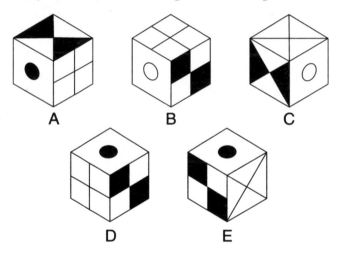

14. Which of the following is not an anagram of a type of weather?

WHORES

TO ADORN

RED HUNT

PET OAK

MY SORT

15.

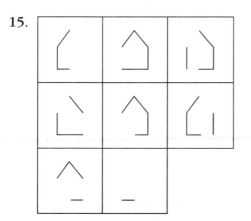

Which is the missing square?

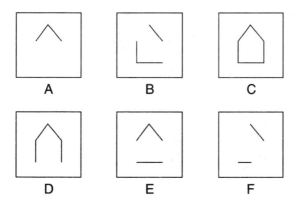

16. Insert the numbers in the boxes in order to make the calculation correct.

$$\boxed{?} \times \boxed{3} - \boxed{?} \div \boxed{9} = \boxed{24}$$

17. Seven synonyms of the keyword PROFICIENT are shown. Take one letter from each of the synonyms in turn to spell out a further synonym of PROFICIENT.

    adept, expert, apt, skilled, competent, able, versed

18. AZDVGRJNM?

    What comes next?

19.  is to: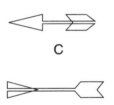

    as

    is to:

A	B	C

D	E	F

20. What number should replace the question mark?

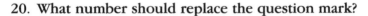

21. Simplify $\dfrac{4}{7} \div \dfrac{16}{35} = x$

22. Replace the letters in the blanks to find LEGAL TERMS.

    – C – U – T – A –

    – A – R – S – E –

    – U – I – I – R –

23. What is the name given to a group of kangaroos?

    a. leap

    b. caste

    c. joey

    d. mob

24. If 33 = 53, what does 23 = ?

25. Find the weight to balance the scale.

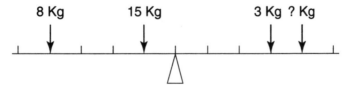

26. Find the word, clockwise or anti-clockwise.

27. Find a nine-letter word by moving from letter to letter. Each letter must be used only once.

O	R	F	C
M	T	E	L
Y	A	S	D
N	X	I	U

28. Move from letter to letter to spell out a 10-letter word. Each letter may be used once only.

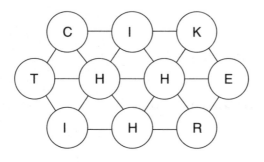

29. What number should replace the ?

30. Which oval is the odd one out?

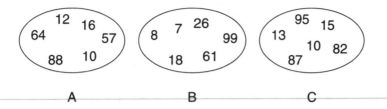

A   B   C

31. Change LARK to BIRD in three steps, one letter at a time.

    LARK

    ——

    ——

    BIRD

32. What is the fear of heaven?

    a. nosophobia

    b. theophobia

    c. uranophobia

    d. acrophobia

33. Which is the odd one out?

    a. IMPALA

    b. CHACMA

    c. CHINCH

    d. AGOUTI

34. Find the word

    - - N R I C K - - - -

35. Solve the REBUS

    # M
    # TOWN
    # AN

36. Fill in the blanks to find two words which are synonyms, clockwise or anti-clockwise.

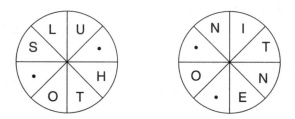

37. Which anagram will not spell out the name of a FOOD?

    a. CUTISIB

    b. GGIIHA

    c. ACEVIAR

    d. CYTHUNE

38. The letters in the circles below have been scrambled. Which circle will not make a six-letter word?

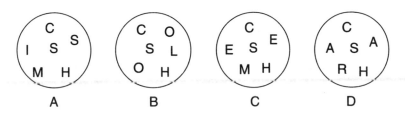

A   B   C   D

39.

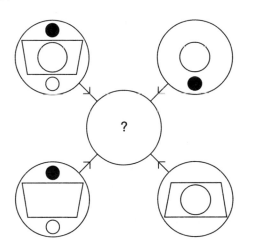

Each line and symbol that appears in the four outer circles above is transferred to the centre circle according to these rules. If a line or symbol occurs in the outer circles:

- once: it is transferred;
- twice: it is possibly transferred;
- three times: it is transferred;
- four times: it is not transferred.

Which of the circles A, B, C, D or E shown below should appear at the centre of the diagram, on page 169?

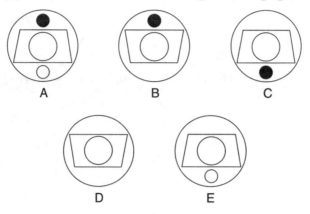

40. Which circle should replace the ? A, B, C or D?

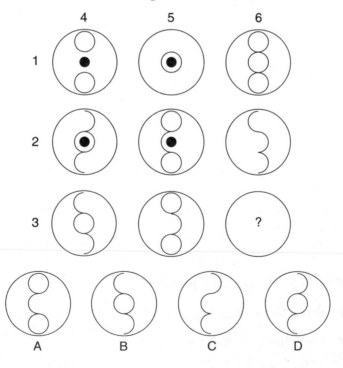

Test Nine: Answers

1. 15

2. fragile, delicate

3. 7; looking across the numbers in identical positions, either increase by two or reduce by two, for example 8, 6, 4 or 3, 5, 7 etc.

4. O; so that a four-letter word can be produced in each quadrant: onus, four, soft, nose.

5. fanlight; it is an English word, the rest being American words.

6. B; in all the others the portion second from the left is repeated second from right.

7. steady

8. 6; there are two alternate sequences starting at seven and four. From seven the sequence progresses +4, +3, +4 etc. From four the sequence progresses –2, +3, –2 etc.

9. D; the rectangle alternates horizontal, vertical. Inside the rectangles is the sequence of four different figures which are inverted second time round.

10. ablution

11. saunter

12. 6486; in all the others the first two digits divided by the third digit is equal to the fourth digit, for example 36/9 = 4.

13. A

14. PET OAK = Topeka. The types of weather are shower (whores), tornado (to adorn), thunder (red hunt) and stormy (my sort).

15. E; looking across and down, the contents of the third square are determined by the first two squares. Only lines which appear once in the first two squares are carried forward. Lines which appear in the same position twice are cancelled out.

16. $74 \times 3 - 6 / 9 = 24$

17. trained

18. J; there are two alternate sequences: AbcDefGhiJklM and ZyxwVutsRqpoNmlkJ.

19. D; the arrow head folds on top of the shaft.

20. 5; each triangular group of three numbers totals 18.

21. $\dfrac{4}{7} \times \dfrac{35}{16} = \dfrac{5}{4} = 1\frac{1}{4}$

22. ACQUITTAL

    BARRISTER

    JUDICIARY

23. d. mob

24. 35 MODULO 6 33 MODULO 10 = 53 MODULO 6

                   23 MODULO 10 = 35 MODULO 6

25. 9½ kg   8 kg × 4 = 32 kg 3 kg × 3   = 9 kg

              15 kg × 1 = 15 kg 9½ kg × 4 = 38 kg

                          47 kg   47 kg

26. sinister

27. taxidermy

28. hitchhiker

29. 12; 62 = 26 reversed, 17 = 71 reversed, 45 = 54 reversed, 94 = 49 reversed, 95 = 59 reversed, 21 = 12 reversed.

30. C

      $6 + 4 = 10$

      $6 + 1 = 7$

      $8 + 7 = 15$

      $8 + 8 = 16$

      $9 + 9 = 18$

      $8 + 2 = 10$

      $5 + 7 = 12$

      $2 + 6 = 8$

      $9 + 5 = 14$ (13)

31. LARK, LARD, BARD, BIRD

32. c. uranophobia

33. c. CHINCH (insect). The others are all animals.

34. jinrickshaw

35. Man about town

36. slothful, indolent

37. b. HAGGII

    a. BISCUIT

    c. CAVIARE

    d. CHUTNEY

38. D

    SCHISM A

    SCHOOL B

    SCHEME C

39. C

40. C; one is added to two to make three. Four is added to five to make six. Similar symbols disappear.

Test Ten: Questions

1.

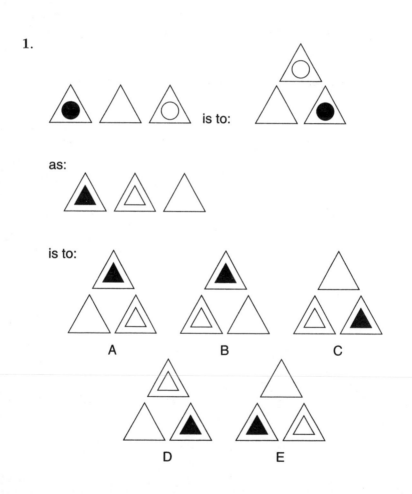

is to:

as:

is to:

A   B   C

D   E

2. Which set of letters is the odd one out?

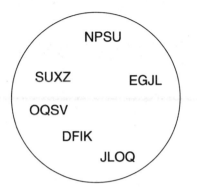

3. Ulna is to arm as mandible is to: cranium, leg, foot, jaw, shoulder.

4. What number should replace the question mark?

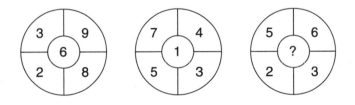

5. Find the starting point and find a 16-letter phrase (2, 6, 8) reading clockwise. Only alternate letters are shown.

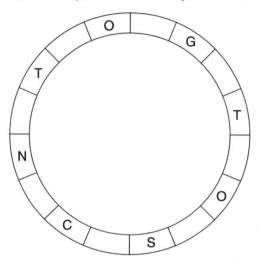

6. Which number is the odd one out?

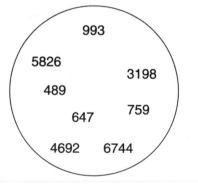

7.

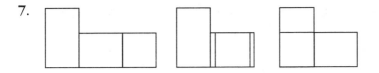

What comes next in the above sequence?

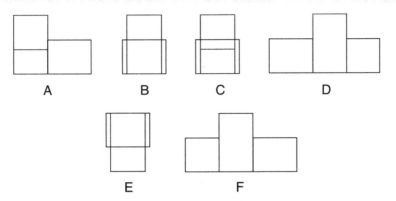

8. What is the longest English word (a type of living creature) that can be produced from the following 10 letters?

MUITBGDAHL

9. What should be the missing number?

382: 115

965: 1514

283: ?

10. Which is the odd one out?

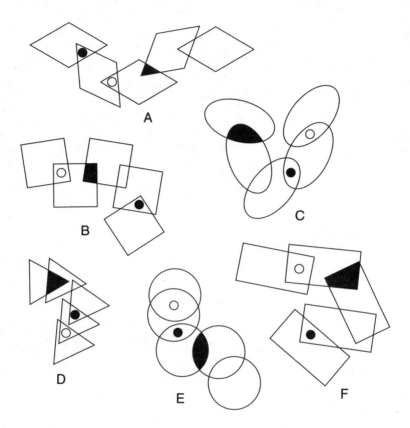

11. Which two rhyming words, which differ by only one letter are synonyms meaning stale?

12. Which of the following is not an anagram of a type of building?

    MAD SUIT

    AM OWED

    ADO GAP

    GET COAT

    EAR GAG

13. Which word in brackets is most opposite in meaning to the word in capitals?

    ITINERANT (calm, random, pleasing, settled, determined).

14.

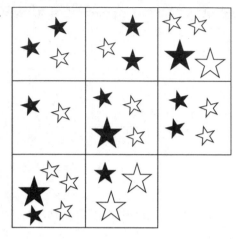

Which is the missing tile?

A

B

C

D

E

F

15.

L	A	E	T	S
Y	T	O	T	E
F	R	A	I	L
A	Y	I	A	L
R	Y	A	W	A

D	N	I	F	S
H	G	U	O	T
I	O	A	N	A
S	O	L	D	I
S	P	E	E	D

Find two words that are synonyms, one in the right-hand grid and one in the left-hand grid. The words may appear horizontally, vertically or diagonally, but always in a straight line.

16. $\dfrac{8124}{4569}$

Change round four digits, two from the top with two from the bottom, to make this fraction equal one half.

17.

What comes next?

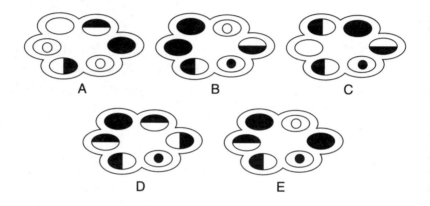

18. Which is the odd one out?

    lexicon, almanac, missal, lectern, thesaurus

19. My watch was correct at 12 noon, after which it began to lose 15 minutes every hour. Eight hours ago it stopped completely. The time showing on my watch is 3.15 pm. What time is it now?

20.

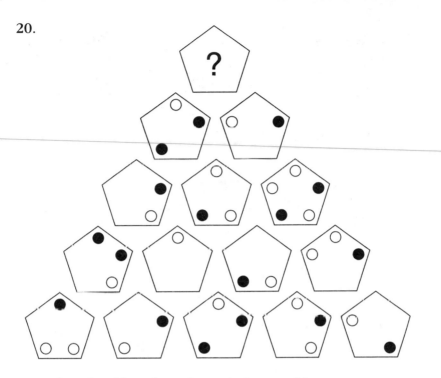

What should replace the question mark?

A   B   C   D   E

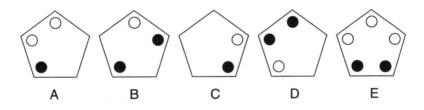

21. Find the single word solution to the following anagram:

DOOR BELL

22. If 17 = 23, what does 27 = ?

23. Simplify $\dfrac{17}{18} \div \dfrac{34}{108} = x$

24. Find a one word solution to the following anagram:

    FLUSTER

25. The combined age of Audrey and Bessie is 16. The combined age of Audrey and Cynthia is 52. The combined age of Bessie and Cynthia is 56. How old are:

    Audrey?

    Bessie?

    Cynthia?

26. Which single word is made up of all the letters in the circles below?

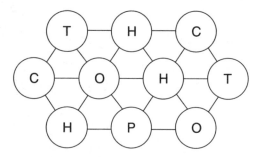

27. All the vowels have been omitted from this trite saying. See if you can replace them.

    DNTBL VNSPR STTNT BRNGS BDLCK

28. Find the word, clockwise or anti-clockwise.

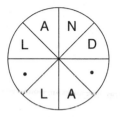

Clue: island

29. What number should replace the ?

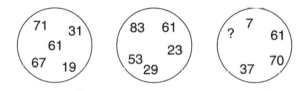

30. Find the highest scoring Scrabble word out of these tiles.

31. Replace the letters in the blanks to form minerals.

– L – M – N – U –

– O – A – S – U –

– A – N – S – U M

32. What is the fear of money?

    a. belonophobia

    b. chrometophobia

    c. monophobia

    d. tropophobia

33. Which is the odd one out?

    a. anabas

    b. chough

    c. drongo

    d. culver

34. Change DATE to LIME in three steps, one letter at a time.

    DATE

    ——

    ——

    LIME

35. How many times must the large cog revolve before all the cogs are back at their starting position?

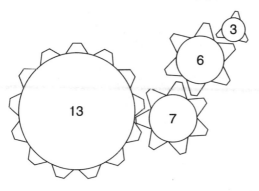

36. The letters in the circles below have been scrambled. Which circle will not make a six-letter word?

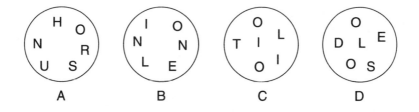

37. Which anagram will not spell out a clothing material?

a. RUCKMAB

b. ROCBADA

c. GINMAGH

d. THEREAL

38. Fill in the blanks to find two words that are synonyms, clockwise or anti-clockwise.

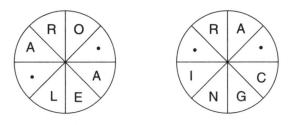

39. Find a word by moving across the circle on the chords and along the circumference.

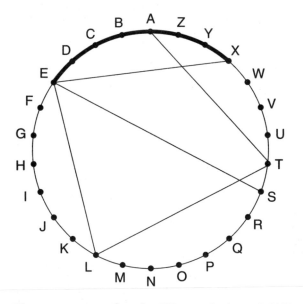

Clue: weapons for the Woman's Army! (10)

40.

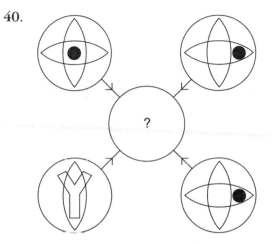

Each line and symbol which appears in the four outer circles above, is transferred to the centre circle according to these rules. If a line or symbol occurs in the outer circles:

- once: it is transferred;
- twice: it is possibly transferred;
- three times: it is transferred;
- four times: it is not transferred.

Which of the circles A, B, C, D or E shown below should appear at the centre of the diagram, above?

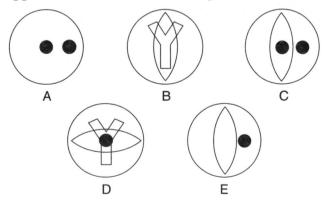

Test Ten: Answers

1. C; the triangle on the right goes to the top, and the other two triangles stay at the bottom but change round.

2. OQSV; it goes in the sequence OpQrStuV; the others go in the sequence NoPqrStU

3. jaw

4. 3; $5 \times 3 = 15$, $6 \times 2 = 12$ and $15 - 12 = 3$. Similarly $7 \times 3 = 21$, $4 \times 5 = 20$ and $21 - 20 = 1$

5. on second thoughts

6. 647; its digits total 17. The digits of all the other numbers total 21.

7. F; the square originally on the right is moving from right to left at each stage.

8. halibut

9. 105; $2 + 8 = 10$, $2 + 3 = 5$

10. E; in all the others the overlapping segments alternate white/black or black/white. In E, two black overlapping segments are adjacent.

11. fusty, musty

12. AM OWED = meadow

    The buildings are: stadium (mad suit), pagoda (ado gap), cottage (get coat) and garage (ear gag).

13. settled

14. E; so that in each row and column there are five black and five white stars.

15. wiry, tough

16. $\dfrac{9164}{4582}$

17. B; when two identical symbols appear in a cloud they disappear and are replaced by two new symbols at the next stage.

18. lectern; it is a reading stand for supporting a book. The rest are all types of book.

19. 1 am

20. A; the contents of each pentagon are determined by the contents of the two pentagons immediately below. Whenever a circle appears in the same corner in the two pentagons below it is not carried forward to the pentagon above, whether two black circles, two black circles or a black and a white circle.

21. bordello

22. 36   17 Mod 10 = 23 Mod 7
        27 Mod 10 = 36 Mod 7

23. $\dfrac{17}{18} \div \dfrac{34}{108} = \dfrac{17}{18} \times \dfrac{108}{34} = \dfrac{6}{2} = 3$

24. restful

25. Audrey 6

    Bessie 10

    Cynthia 46

26. hotchpotch

27. Don't believe in superstition it brings bad luck.

28. Falkland

29. 74; each circle adds to 249.

30. muzzle (26)

31. aluminium, potassium, magnesium

32. chrometophobia

33. a. anabas (fish). The remainder are birds.

34. date, dame, dime, lime

35. 42

36. C

 A: ONRUSH, B: ONLINE, D: OODLES

37. b

 a. BUCKRAM

 c. GINGHAM

 d. LEATHER

38. adorable, charming

39. battleaxes

40. D

THE ⚜ TIMES

TESTING SERIES

Published by Kogan Page Interactive, The Times Testing Series is an exciting new range of interactive CD-ROMs that will provide invaluable practice tests for job applicants and for those seeking a brain-stretching challenge.

Each CD-ROM features:

- hundreds of unique interactive questions
- instant scoring with feedback and analysis
- hours of practice and fun
- questions devised by top UK MENSA puzzle editors and test experts
- against-the-clock, real test conditions
- a program that allows users to create their own tests

Brain Teasers
Volume 1

Brain Teasers Volume 1 is a quick, efficient and reliable way to develop essential problem-solving skills. This CD-ROM contains hundreds of brain teaser puzzles and allows the user to:

- introduce stress factors and time constraints

- receive valuable interactive feedback

- develop problem-solving skills

- have fun by pitting their wits against mind-stretching questions and puzzles

Psychometric Tests
Volume 1

Psychometric Tests Volume 1 provides essential practice for any job applicant who has to face a selection test.

With this CD-ROM users will be able to:

- practise on tests based on those used by top employers

- learn how to tackle different types of questions

- experience real test conditions

- receive instant results and invaluable feedback

THE TIMES

TESTING SERIES

Test Your IQ
Volume 1

This interactive CD-ROM contains hundreds of questions just like those used in job selection IQ tests. *Test Your IQ* Volume 1 enables users to:

- practise for hours and achieve improved scores

- score against their friends

- develop their vocabulary and powers of logic

- practise on randomly selected tests every time

Test Your Aptitude
Volume 1

By working through the tests contained in this interactive CD-ROM users will get a clear insight into what really makes them tick and the sort of job that would suit them best. *Test Your Aptitude* Volume 1 will reveal to users:

- what really motivates them

- which career best suits their personality

- their strengths and weaknesses

- how they will perform in selection tests

Available in March 2002 from all good bookshops, software outlets and the Kogan Page Web site. To obtain further information, please contact the publisher at the address below:

Kogan Page Ltd
120 Pentonville Road
London N1 9JN
Tel: 020 7278 0433
Fax: 020 7837 6348

www.kogan-page.co.uk